THE MOST
BIZARRE TRUE
CRIME STORIES
EVER TOLD

Free Bonus Books

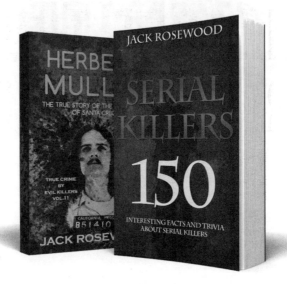

Get two free True Crime books when you
join Jack Rosewood's newsletter over at
www.JackRosewood.com/free

THE MOST BIZARRE TRUE CRIME STORIES EVER TOLD

JACK ROSEWOOD

SPHERE

SPHERE

First published in Great Britain in 2023 by Sphere

5 7 9 10 8 6 4

A CIP catalogue record for this book
is available from the British Library.

ISBN 978-1-4087-3108-6

Typeset in Garamond by M Rules
Printed and bound in Great Britain by
Clays Ltd, Elcograf S.p.A.

Papers used by Sphere are from well-managed forests
and other responsible sources.

Sphere
An imprint of
Little, Brown Book Group
Carmelite House
50 Victoria Embankment
London EC4Y 0DZ

The authorised representative
in the EEA is
Hachette Ireland
8 Castlecourt Centre
Dublin 15, D15 XTP3, Ireland
(email: info@hbgi.ie)

An Hachette UK Company
www.hachette.co.uk

www.littlebrown.co.uk

Contents

Introduction

With the massive wave of true crime content that has been produced over the last decade, even those who aren't interested in the macabre seem to know the gruesome details of the major cases in the crime realm. The heavy hitters are a little played out at this point. By the time a streaming service makes an eight-part TV drama about a 'shocking' true crime story, it's usually already old news to the die-hard crime devotee. They call it a riveting tale with twists you'll never see coming; meanwhile, crime junkies have already read all the books, watched the news coverage, and heard every detail of the story from about ten different podcasts. Simple murder has become mundane. Where's the weird? Where are the one-off cases that don't get the Bundy treatment? Where's the truly creepy stuff that makes you think twice about turning off the light?

While the Night Stalkers, BTKs, and Killer Clowns of the

1

world can still provide some graphic nightmare fuel, real true crime lovers are either left underwhelmed by the straightforward nature of their crimes or have heard the details so many times that they have lost their impact. The most intense fans of the genre are looking for something new. We want to be genuinely shocked, deeply disturbed, and left wondering if anyone or anything is safe.

That's exactly what this collection of stories aims to do. In *The Most Bizarre True Crime Stories Ever Told* you'll find utterly odd cases that contain some seriously strange details that go beyond the run-of-the-mill murders everyone has heard of.

This book includes tales of cannibals, one of whom proudly walked free in search of new victims; a seemingly impossible account of a dead woman who solved her own murder; bone-chilling stories of killers hiding in family homes, unbeknownst to the people living there; and several morbid mysteries that have such heart-pounding twists and turns they seem like they were stolen right off the big screen from a Hollywood thriller. Like all great true crime stories, these cases also delve deep into human nature, love, loneliness, fear, and the absurdity of the justice system.

So lock your doors, close the blinds, and keep an ear out for someone who might be living in your walls, because you're about to go on a journey through the most bizarre true crime stories that will creep out even the most desensitized of fans.

Armin Meiwes, The Rotenburg Cannibal

M eeting someone online and having them over for dinner sounds like a perfectly normal story of modern dating, but when Armen Meiwes met Bernd Jürgen Brandes on a message board, neither man was simply looking to uncork a bottle of wine and begin a romance. What transpired after that meeting turned out to be a fascinating case, blurring the lines of fantasy, morality, and the very nature of consent.

Armin Meiwes was born on December 1, 1961 in Kassel, Germany, the last of three boys. As a child, he was obsessed with the fairy tale *Hansel and Gretel*, a German story about a witch living in the woods who tries to cook and eat two abandoned children who trespass into her candy-coated cottage.

Meiwes's family moved to a massive thirty-six-room farmhouse in Rotenburg where he ran around with his brothers, rode horses, and played on the huge estate. He described his early childhood as 'lovely.'

According to Meiwes's recollection, when he was eight years old, his parents divorced and his father left the family, taking all their money with him. He remembers seeing his father drive away, and running after him, screaming for him to stop while his father stared straight ahead and ignored his young, distraught son. When Meiwes's two older brothers also left the home, he began dealing with deep feelings of abandonment, and tremendous pressure to be the 'man of the house.'

Meiwes recalls creating an imaginary brother he named Franky, to whom he would tell all his darkest secrets. He desperately wanted someone to be with him forever, someone who could not abandon him, and he frequently had fantasies about consuming others' flesh so they would always be with him.

His mother, now thrice divorced, was domineering and extremely overbearing. She berated Meiwes in public and would go with him everywhere. If women were ever interested in Meiwes, she would chase them away. She lived a rich fantasy life, dressing up in medieval costumes, and decorating her expansive estate to match.

At eighteen, Meiwes joined the army, where he did exceedingly well, and was promoted several times. He had a community, a real brotherhood, for the first time in his life, and his fantasies of consuming people subsided for the twelve years that he served. Despite his successes, he was eventually discharged from the services. He went to live with his aging mother in the farmhouse where he had grown up and started working as a computer technician.

In 1996, Meiwes's mother was injured in a car accident. He was already her caretaker, but she became almost impossible to live with once she was practically bed bound. She became more demanding after her accident.

In 1999 she died, leaving Meiwes alone in the expansive and remote family home. Free from the structure of the army, and the tyranny of his mother, Meiwes was finally able to do what he wanted. He began looking at brutal torture and pain pornography. Despite the graphic nature of the videos he watched, he was still not satisfied. His childhood fantasies of consuming others were still lurking in the back of his mind. Eventually, Meiwes made his way to websites and message boards devoted to finding people who wanted to be killed and eaten.

In 2000, Meiwes posted on the website Cannibal Cafe that he was 'looking for a young, well-built man aged 18 to 30 years old to slaughter and consume.'

Meiwes later alleged he received around two hundred serious applicants for his post, all willing to be killed and eaten. He met up with several young men wanting to experience being killed and eaten, but most left the meetings after getting cold feet. Meiwes never wanted to do anything without the person's enthusiastic and free consent, however, so whenever one of his potential victims hesitated even slightly, he lost interest and let them go.

A hotel worker by the name of Dirk Moeller later testified that he had met with Meiwes, who had chained him up, and per Moeller's request, pinned pieces of paper to his body that denoted what cut of meat each section would be, as you would do to an animal before butchery. Moeller changed his mind about being killed and was freely let go by Meiwes without any trouble. He only wanted willing victims.

Meanwhile, Bernd Jürgen Brandes, a forty-three-year-old computer engineer, was also perusing Cannibal Cafe, looking to be eaten by a cannibal.

His post read 'Dinner—or your dinner' in which he promised the reader they'd get 'the chance to eat [him] alive.' Brandes had a troubled life. His mother committed suicide when he was five, and his father had shut down and refused to discuss it. Later, when Brandes came out as gay, Brandes alleges his father stopped talking to him.

Brandes had a significant pain fetish and would pay sex workers to satisfy his needs. One man said Brandes had offered him all his belongings and money for him to bite his penis off.

On February 14, 2001, Brandes got a message from Meiwes, replying to his post on the message board. The pair exchanged messages for a few weeks, discussing boundaries, and detailing how Meiwes would kill Brandes, how he would eat him, and what should be done with the rest of his body afterward.

On March 9, 2001, Brandes took an early morning train from Berlin. At 11:14 a.m., he got off the train and met the man who would eventually kill him. Meiwes recalls being 'nervous and excited' when he first laid eyes on Brandes, and later described him as 'a very nice, lovely man.'

The loud, busy train station made for an awkward first meeting place. The two yelled their hellos as best they could over the hustle and bustle of regular people taking their every-day train journeys who could have no idea about the sinister reason these two seemingly normal men were meeting. The hour-long ride back to Meiwes's home gave them time to relax into each other's company. Brandes was apparently very comfortable by the time they reached their destination, as he stripped naked almost as soon as they entered the house. Meiwes recalls that Brandes wanted him to 'admire dinner.'

On the second floor, Meiwes had constructed a 'slaughter room' complete with a bed, a butchery table, and a meat hook. They lay on the bed chatting and touching one another. Meiwes said they had sex because Brandes wanted to, but nei-ther of them was that enthusiastic about it. Brandes quickly realized Meiwes didn't have the strength or inclination to inflict the pain on him that he really needed.

After that disappointment, Brandes seemed to change his mind about the whole thing. Meiwes was once again facing the possibility of having his fantasy slip through his fingers, but he was not at all interested in forcing anyone to do any-thing. As soon as consent was removed, Meiwes soured on the situation and no longer wanted to go through with it. He agreed to drive Brandes back to the train station.

At the station, though, Brandes changed his mind back.

He requested they stop in town for some sleeping pills and cough medicine that he thought might dull his sensation and calm his mind enough for Meiwes to be able to go through with the original plan.

Back at the farmhouse, around 6:30 p.m., Brandes anxiously said to Meiwes, 'I can't stand it anymore. Cut it off.'

Meiwes set up his camcorder to record the night and set to work attempting to remove Brandes's penis. The first knife he used was too dull. The second made quick work of the amputation. Meiwes said Brandes 'screamed horribly,' but it only lasted twenty to thirty seconds.

Meiwes's lawyer Harald Ermel, who later had the macabre task of studying the four-hour video made that night, said he could tell that Brandes was very much enjoying the fountain of blood spurting out of the open wound where his penis used to be.

The two men had already agreed that they would share the member as Brandes's last meal. Meiwes cut it in half, blanched the pieces, and pan-fried them with salt, pepper, and garlic powder. Unfortunately for them, the pieces shriveled up and became inedible.

Around 9 p.m., Brandes began feeling very cold from blood loss, so Meiwes ran him a hot bath and went to another room to read a *Star Trek* novel while waiting for Brandes to pass away. Hours passed, and Brandes was still alive. Meiwes went to check on him at about 11:30 p.m. to find him woozy but 'happy, because he was lying in his own blood.'

Eventually, Brandes wanted to get out of the bath. He was

so badly weakened he could barely stand, and he soon collapsed onto the floor. He spent the next several hours in the slaughter room coming in and out of consciousness.

At around 2:30 a.m. on the morning of March 10, Brandes once again collapsed to the floor unconscious after trying to get out of bed. The tape of the night showed Meiwes distraught and clearly unsure of what to do. He picked up and put down a knife several times. He later said he thought about calling for an ambulance but was stopped by how close he was to the fulfillment of his lifelong desire to butcher and eat a person.

Meiwes even prayed for guidance on what to do next, though he admits he didn't know if he 'should pray to the Devil or God.' He also says he asked God for forgiveness for what he was about to do. After a lot more hesitation, Meiwes eventually cut Brandes's throat, finally bringing his life, plagued with morbid sexual fetishes and dark fantasies of being eaten alive, to a sobering end.

Meiwes was now free to fulfill his equally dark fantasies. The internet had provided him with all the information he needed to butcher a human. Meiwes decapitated Brandes, hung him on the meat hook in the slaughter room, removed his organs, and cut his body in half. The pieces were cut into meal-sized chunks, with Meiwes mentally labeling the pieces as you would a cow in a slaughterhouse.

His first meal made from Brandes's body consisted of 'a piece of rump steak—a piece from his back,' which he ate in a candle-lit room, on his best dinnerware, along with a lovely

9

red wine, potatoes, and Brussels sprouts. He kept the rest of the body in a false-bottom freezer in his kitchen, underneath cuts of other, non-human meat.

Meiwes said Brandes tasted 'like pork, but stronger' and that he very much enjoyed the flavor. However, the taste wasn't all he was interested in. Consuming another was always a pathway to true bonding and a deep connection. He said later, 'I was getting the feeling that I was actually achieving this perfect inner connection through his flesh,' and that since consuming Brandes, 'he is always with me.'

Meiwes buried the inedible parts of Brandes's body in his garden and set out to find another willing victim as he worked his way through the meat in his freezer. Again, he posted on Cannibal Cafe, and again, he got a lot of interest.

In November 2002, an Austrian student got in touch, curious about Meiwes's history and experience. Meiwes didn't go into detail but told him that he 'wouldn't be the first.' The student got a weird feeling that Meiwes was actually telling the truth and was keeping a dark secret, so he called the authorities.

On December 11, 2002, police raided the farmhouse and found fifteen pounds of Brandes's body still untouched in the freezer, as well as the videotape Meiwes had recorded that night.

On July 17, 2003, Meiwes was charged with murder and brought to court, after being judged sane and fit to stand trial. The case proved difficult for prosecutors because cannibalism is not actually illegal in Germany. The tape, and the correspondence between the two men, also clearly showed that Brandes was a willing victim who seemed to enjoy what happened to him.

Meiwes pushed for being convicted of 'killing on demand,' a kind of euthanasia that, while not totally legal, only carried a five-year jail sentence. He said, 'I wanted to eat him but I didn't want to kill him,' and reiterated that 'Bernd came to [him] of his own free will to end his life.'

On January 30, 2004, Armin Meiwes was convicted of manslaughter and sentenced to eight and a half years in prison.

In April 2005, the prosecution called for a retrial, claiming Meiwes should have been charged with murder. During the trial that began on January 12, 2006, lawyers argued that Brandes could not have consented to the acts due to his level of intoxication and that there was no way around the fact that Meiwes was the one who ended Brandes's life. This time the verdict was not so lenient. Meiwes was convicted of murder and given a life sentence.

Meiwes says he regrets what he did and would not do it again given the opportunity.

To people with similar inclinations, he gave this advice, which seems to imply that he was not satisfied by carrying out the macabre dream he had wished for his entire life: 'The wishes, the fantasies you have can never, ever be fulfilled, and everything that you dream about will always remain a dream.'

Sources say he is now a vegetarian.

Missy Bevers and the SWAT Murderer

On Monday, April 18, 2016, Missy Bevers woke in the very early hours to get ready and drive to Creekside Church in Midlothian, Texas. She arrived at 4:18 a.m. and began hauling exercise equipment into the church's indoor classroom. The wife and mother of three girls was setting up for a popular 5 a.m. Camp Gladiator bootcamp class. Those who attended her class regularly said Missy was an energetic and motivating presence that made them look forward to the early exercise classes.

Students began arriving just before 5 a.m., but instead of finding Missy ready to give her beloved students a dynamic workout, they found her lying face up on the floor of the classroom, surrounded by broken glass from an unknown source.

The frantic students called 911 at 5:06 a.m., but there was nothing that could be done; Missy was already dead.

Police immediately began an investigation, and it wasn't long before an extremely promising lead presented itself. While, unfortunately, the cameras in the church's parking lot had been out of service for some time, the interior of the church was equipped with motion-sensor security cameras.

At around 3:50 a.m. that morning the cameras had been activated. They caught a clear picture of the murderer wandering the halls.

The individual was dressed head to toe in black police riot gear, complete with a black face covering, a helmet with a light attached to it, and what looked to be a bullet-proof vest with large white letters spelling out *POLICE* across the back and chest. They seemed eerily calm and in control as they stalked the halls of the church, checking doors and breaking things with the hammer that was clutched in their left hand.

The medical examiner later said, 'the wounds on Missy's head and chest were consistent with the tool the suspect was carrying,' though police have not released exactly how Missy died.

The authorities studied the tape to get an accurate profile of the suspect. They said the individual was between five feet two inches and five feet eight inches, and walked with a distinctive gait; with their toes pointed outward, and a slight limp or lilt to their walk. Interestingly, the authorities said the walk had a 'feminine sway' and, considering how short the suspect was, they could not rule out the possibility that the killer was a woman.

Because the security tape showed that the suspect was

already in the building by the time Missy arrived, the first theory was that she had accidentally interrupted a burglary in progress and was murdered in a panic.

However, this wasn't a so-called Mega Church known to use expensive AV equipment or be raking in huge donations. Creekside was a relatively small church, especially by Texas standards, that served the small town of Midlothian. Maybe a desperate person looking to do a quick smash-and-grab would target a church for whatever they could find, but the person caught on camera did not look like a frenzied small-time criminal. There's also the fact that nothing of value was taken. Church officials said none of their equipment was missing, and even Missy's jewelry was left untouched. So if it wasn't a robbery, what was it? Was Missy specifically targeted?

Of course, the police did what they always do in these cases, and turned their attention to Missy's husband. Brandon Bevers fully cooperated with the police. He gave them access to everything they needed and didn't seem to be hiding anything. Brandon told them his twenty-year marriage had been solid, and he didn't know anybody who even disliked Missy, let alone anyone who would want to kill her. Brandon also had an air-tight alibi for the night his wife was murdered. He was on a fishing trip in Mississippi, which police were able to confirm through receipts and surveillance footage.

On April 22, four days after the murder, the authorities thought they had a massive break in the case. A man had taken a white, blood-stained, woman's long-sleeved shirt into a dry cleaner in Midlothian. He claimed it was canine blood from a dog fight he'd broken up in his daughter's backyard, after which he'd had to take his dog to the emergency vet.

The dry cleaner knew of the shocking murder that had occurred just four days before. He called the police, not only because he was suspicious of the man's story, but because that man was Randy Bevers, Missy's father-in-law. What was a member of Missy's family doing with a blood-stained garment only a few days after her murder?

Speculation spread wildly as the public got its hands on this information. A theory sprung up that Brandon and his father were working together, and Brandon had just taken his fishing trip as a cover for his whereabouts while his father committed a crime they knew Brandon would be suspected of. Others thought Randy had worked alone to try and get Brandon out of a bad marriage without losing any money or custody of his daughters in a bitter divorce.

It didn't help Randy's case that he also matched the physical description of the suspect from the surveillance footage to a T. He was a shorter, stocky man, and walked with his toes pointed outward; the same distinctive gait used by the suspect in the surveillance footage.

Unfortunately for those who thought they had solved the mystery, all of Randy's alibis checked out. He had been on a golfing trip in California on the morning of Missy's murder. His daughter Christie also confirmed that a dog fight *had* happened in her backyard, and there was surveillance footage from the emergency vet that showed Randy did indeed take his dog to be treated after the fight.

People in the community held out hope that the blood on the shirt from the dry cleaner would still come back a match to Missy's, or at least become another promising lead, but it was confirmed to be canine blood.

The family bore no ill will toward the dry cleaner or the community who speculated about the Bevers's involvement in Missy's death. In fact, they held a press conference and thanked everyone involved for bringing whatever they could to the authorities. They encouraged people to keep looking out for anything suspicious that may lead to a suspect.

When police received the records back from Missy and Brandon's phones, they found evidence of the couple having marital problems due to both financial struggles and infidelity. This didn't necessarily mean that Brandon was lying to the police about their happy marriage, but it did open up the possibility that Missy had been messing around with someone who may have been dangerous, or maybe that the killer was related to someone looking for revenge, such as a scorned spouse.

Police followed up on several more leads surrounding the possible infidelity that was alluded to in the Beverses' text messages. A friend of Missy's recalled Missy showing her a 'creepy' message she had received from an unknown man on her LinkedIn profile just a few days before she was killed. The authorities looked into the rest of Missy's activities on LinkedIn. They couldn't find the specific message Missy's friend remembered, but did find what they called 'flirty and familiar' messages and even some that turned 'intimate.'

A workout buddy of Missy's named Mark also said that she was acting unusually around the time she was killed, and some sources say she even suddenly stopped going to the gym she had gone to almost daily for years. Could someone have been following her?

The problem with being an independent contractor for a fitness business is that your business relies on advertising. You have to let people know where you will be almost every single day. Missy had posted on her Facebook page the day before her murder that, even if the expected rain did ruin her plan for an outdoor bootcamp, the class would still be meeting inside the church. If someone wanted to know where Missy was, all they had to do was look at her social media. Striking before an extremely early workout class would ensure that it was dark, Missy was alone, and most of the town was still asleep.

However, some people don't believe that Missy thought she was in danger. She lived in Texas, an open-carry state, and did have a gun registered to her name. She had left that gun in her car as she set up for the class that day, leading many to believe that Missy wasn't expecting anything to happen to her. After all, if you were scared for your life, and setting up alone in a dark, desolate area before the sun even crested the horizon, you would probably bring a form of protection, right?

Once again the trail went cold as investigators ruled out the persons of interest from Missy's LinkedIn messages, call logs, and text messages.

Looking to the public for help, police released a video from the night of the murder showing an extremely suspicious vehicle. They concluded that it was a silver Nissan Altima made between 2010 and 2012, with an oval sticker on the back. The car entered the parking lot of a sporting goods store down the block from the church at 1:58 a.m., turned off its lights, and very slowly circled the parking lot. It stopped for a moment, turned its lights on and off several more times, and left the lot at 2:04 a.m., less than two hours before the unknown suspect entered Creekside Church.

No useful leads came from this information, but another vehicle became the next point of interest for police. At around 4:30 on the morning of the murder, a witness said they saw a dark SUV leaving the church parking lot. This wasn't much information to go on, but once again, the community proved helpful.

Since Missy's murder, police had received more than a thousand tips about various aspects of the case and suspicious people who should be investigated. Many of those tips were about a man named Bobby Wayne Henry. Bobby drove a brown SUV similar to the one the witness saw that night. He was also a former police officer and tactical agent, who admitted to the investigators that he still owned some of his tactical gear, though he said it no longer fit.

Bobby had been fired from the force in 1996 for aggravated sexual assault and had since been working as a security guard. He also attended Creekside Church, where Missy was murdered, and had actually worked security at her funeral, as it was such a high-profile case. It certainly wouldn't be the first time a killer had attended their victim's funeral. It's fairly common for a criminal to want to return to the scene of the crime or check up on the aftermath of what they have done. The community was disturbed and disgusted to think that maybe Missy's murderer may not only have been there but had actually been paid to attend her funeral.

Those who called the police about Bobby had also noted that the man had an extremely distinctive gait, just like the suspect on the tapes. The authorities even brought in a forensic podiatrist to compare Bobby's gait to that of the suspect, but they could not definitively conclude that they were the same.

Police seriously looked into Bobby, but, other than the inconclusive report on the strange gait, there were several reasons they couldn't match him to the person who murdered Missy. First of all, he was over six feet tall, while they believed the suspect on the security cameras to be between five foot two inches and five foot eight inches. He also passed several polygraph tests, and his wife said he was home with her all night and into the morning that the crime occurred.

The investigation didn't clear Bobby of everything, though. The authorities found child pornography on his computer, and he was arrested and jailed in 2017. Bobby was the last major lead in the case.

Despite the suspect being caught on camera, a suspicious vehicle acting oddly right down the street from the murder, reports of 'creepy' messages from strangers, and many tips that led to a former police tactical agent with the same strange walk as the suspect, this case has never been solved.

Carl Tanzler and
His Eternal Love Story

If there is a fine line between love and obsession, Carl Tanzler tip-toed across that line and then proceeded to run as fast as he could for several miles.

Carl Tanzler was born in 1877 in Germany. Not much is known about his early life. In his early forties, he married and had two children. In 1926, he moved his family to Zephyrhills, Florida, outside Tampa. He then abandoned his family and went to work as a radiologic technician at Marine Hospital in Key West, under the new name Count Carl von Cosel.

Despite not having the credentials to do so, Carl began treating a beautiful twenty-two-year-old Cuban American woman named Maria Elena Milagro de Hoyos, known as Elena. Carl was immediately smitten with Elena and not just because she was young and beautiful.

Carl claimed that throughout his adolescence he'd had visions of family members who would show him his true love. These matchmaking ghosts allegedly showed him a gorgeous, dark-featured woman. When Carl saw Elena, he knew she was the woman he had been waiting for all his life.

Elena was at the hospital to be treated for tuberculosis which, at the time, was a terminal diagnosis.

Carl was devastated that he'd just met the love of his life, and she was going to be taken from him so soon. He was determined to save her so the two could be together, like in his fantasies. Tanzler began treating Elena at her Key West home, creating homemade tinctures, tonics, and medicines to try and cure her.

He became close with her family, but it is unknown whether they knew of his romantic intent or thought he was just a very attentive doctor. All the while he was treating Elena, he was also professing his love for her and showering her with gifts, though Elena did not reciprocate the love of this fifty-plus-year-old man who was so obsessed with her.

Despite Carl's many attempts to create the elixir of life, on October 25, 1931, Elena succumbed to her tuberculosis and passed away. Carl offered to pay for the construction of a custom mausoleum in Key West Cemetery. He ended up having the only key to the building.

For two years, Carl visited Elena's grave every night. One night in 1933, he suddenly stopped showing up, which aroused some suspicion from the family and cemetery workers, but nothing that caused too much worry. They thought maybe he had lost interest in his love for Elena or that he was simply too busy to continue a nightly pilgrimage to her resting place.

In fact, Carl had eliminated the need to visit his beloved's grave every night by removing her body from the mausoleum and taking it to his home in a toy wagon. Because Carl had made sure he was the only one with a key to the mausoleum, nobody realized Elena was missing.

Tanzler had spent the two years since Elena's death constructing a rudimentary laboratory inside an old airplane. It was complete with supplies to slow a body's decomposition and keep its decaying flesh intact. He used silk covered in mortician's wax and papier mâché to keep Elena's face looking as normal as possible. He also stuffed her torso with rags to keep it shapely, and gave her glass eyes, because her own had decomposed. Tanzler rammed wire coat hangers into her limbs as makeshift bones, to maintain the body's structure.

To stave off the smell of decomposition, he covered the body in flowers, perfumes, and disinfectants. Because her scalp was rotting, he had even constructed a wig for her, made from her own hair, which he had received from Elena's mother. Tanzler slept in the same bed as Elena's corpse for the next seven years.

Over these seven years, people around the town started becoming suspicious of Tanzler. He kept coming into boutiques to buy women's clothes and jewelry, but he was never actually seen with a woman. He was known to be a recluse, and nobody thought he was married, or even seeing anyone. So who or what was he buying all this finery for?

A young boy cycling past Tanzler's remote home also reported that he saw him dancing with what the boy thought was a life-sized doll.

Rumors of his strange behavior reached the de Hoyos family, leading Elena's sister, Florinda, to drop in on Tanzler in 1940. She initially also thought the figure was just a doll of her sister. She found it unsettling but didn't think there was any possibility it was actually her sister's body. Elena had been dead for seven years, and, as far as she knew, was still lying in her mausoleum in Key West Cemetery. Florinda alerted the authorities anyway, though, because she felt so uncomfortable with the figure she had seen in Tanzler's home.

The authorities went to Tanzler's isolated home and found the 'doll' that the boy and Elena's sister had spoken of. After some tests, they concluded it was, in fact, Elena's body. Among all the other alterations to her body, they found a cardboard tube placed in her groin as a makeshift vagina. Investigators said they couldn't determine whether Tanzler had used it for sexual gratification or just for structural integrity, though it could have been just too shocking and depraved a detail to release to the public in the forties.

Tanzler was arrested for grave robbing and found mentally competent to stand trial despite some obviously unhinged things he swore happened. First, he said that Elena's spirit would visit him every night while he sat next to her body in her mausoleum. He said she told him she wanted Carl to take her from her resting place and live with him.

Second, he said he had planned 'to use an airship to take Elena high into the stratosphere so that radiation from outer space could penetrate her tissues and restore life to her somnolent form.'

Horrifyingly, the statute of limitations for grave robbing had already been reached, and Carl Tanzler was allowed to go free without facing any consequences for the horrific and dehumanizing modifications he had made to Elena's body.

The horror continued, as Elena's body was put on display for the curious onlookers who had heard about the morbid case in the news. She was shown at the Dean-Lopez Funeral Home, and seven thousand people came to see her before she was finally put to rest in an unmarked grave in Key West Cemetery.

Tanzler died alone in 1952 in his Florida home.

Teresita Basa, The Woman Who Solved Her Own Murder

The most tragic and frustrating part of a homicide with no witnesses is that nobody will ever know what really happened: how the victim spent their last moments, whether they knew their killer had bad intentions, or if they were aware they were in danger before being dealt their death blow.

Teresita Basa's friends and family experienced this confusion and grief, while racking their brains for any useful information, after she was the victim of a brutal murder. Almost six months went by with no leads—that is, until Teresita herself decided to step in and give the authorities exactly what they needed.

Teresita Basa was born in 1929, in the Philippines, to wealthy parents Pedro and Soccoro Basa. She was well educated, well traveled, and an extremely talented musician. She graduated from a university in Manila and moved to the U.S.A. in the sixties to continue her education.

Teresita enrolled in a Master's program in Chicago to study music. She eventually decided to pivot her career focus and use her smarts and people skills to work as a respiratory therapist at Edgewater Hospital, the birthplace of both politician Hillary Clinton and serial killer John Wayne Gacy.

Teresita offered piano lessons on weekends while she worked toward her degree.

On February 23, 1977, Teresita left work at 5:30 p.m., arrived at her friend Ruth Loeb's apartment, and spoke to Ruth for half an hour. Ruth said that Teresita told her she was expecting a friend, possibly a gentleman caller, but Ruth got no other identifying details about the man.

At around 8:40 p.m. that night, Teresita's neighbors on the fifteenth floor of their Chicago apartment, Katherine and Marid Knazze, smelled smoke coming from somewhere on their floor. They alerted the building caretaker, who called the fire department. When they arrived, they quickly tracked down the smell to Teresita's apartment.

Initially, the first responders thought it would be a routine apartment fire from a kitchen mishap or an out-of-control candle, but firefighters found a much more gruesome scene than the expected overcooked dinner.

Amid the billowing smoke, forty-seven-year-old Teresita was found nude, with a knife sticking out of her chest, under a mattress that had been set on fire. The authorities were obviously dealing with a homicide. It did not appear that she had been sexually assaulted, so the fact that she was naked was a strange detail.

The investigation didn't turn up many leads, except a small note, scribbled in pen, saying: 'Get theater tickets for A.S.'

Months passed without any leads, any motivations, or any suspects. Who would want to harm Teresita at all, let alone in such a violent manner, and in a large apartment building where any number of witnesses could have seen them? It obviously looked like an intimate crime of passion, but Teresita was not known to have been dating anybody and never mentioned anybody acting strangely to her family or friends. As an immigrant from the Philippines, Teresita had connected with many other ex-pats from her country in the States and had quite a few friends she spoke to regularly. None of them mentioned Teresita feeling uneasy prior to her death.

The case was in danger of growing cold and passing into obscurity; that is, until Detective Joseph Stachula arrived at work to find an interesting note on his desk. It directed him to contact the Evanston police department about the Basa case. When he called them, they told him to call a co-worker and friend of Teresita's. Stachula was about to hear an entirely unbelievable tale.

When Stachula and his partner Lee Epplen called the number, they reached Jose C. Chua Jr., a doctor at Edgewater Hospital, who told them that his wife, Remibias 'Remy' Chua, had been having disturbing dreams for several weeks.

Shortly after Teresita's death, Remy awoke, distressed, having dreamed about her friend detailing her own murder, including who had done it. Unfortunately, as with most dreams, the details began to fade the moment woke up. Remy was certain that these dreams weren't just fabrications of her subconscious and was extremely distraught that she couldn't remember everything Teresita had said, so she could help her friend get justice. Dr. Chua assumed his wife was simply grieving her deceased friend and experiencing nightmares.

Then things changed.

When Remy was taking a nap one day, she started speaking to Dr. Chua as if in a trance, in a voice that wasn't hers. The voice said 'Ako'y Teresita Basa,' meaning 'I am Teresita Basa' in their native language of Tagalog. Dr. Chua was shocked and scared, especially since his wife said that she didn't remember anything about the trance when she awoke.

Again, he hoped it was some form of extreme grief working itself out while his wife slept. However, the trances continued. The voice said to him, 'Doctor, I would like to ask for your help. The man who murdered me is still at large.' The voice claiming to be Teresita continued to visit Dr. Chua, telling him exactly who had killed her and how.

He said the Teresita voice 'told me I had nothing to be scared of' and that 'she was really pleading for me to help solve her murder.'

Dr. Chua was extremely hesitant to contact the authorities about a paranormal occurrence. As a man of science, he was conflicted about implicating anyone based on such strange evidence. How could he genuinely go to the authorities and say that the ghost of Teresita Basa had told him who had murdered her from beyond the grave? It was truly absurd, and surely wouldn't be taken seriously.

Then Teresita possessed Remy again, asking Dr. Chua why he hadn't contacted the police yet. He let the voice know his concerns; that without any actual evidence, his claim would be mocked and dismissed. Teresita seemed to understand where Dr. Chua was coming from, so she gave him some concrete information he could take to the police.

The voice told him that her murderer had stolen several pieces of jewelry from her and gave him the names and telephone numbers of four family members who could confirm that these pieces belonged to Teresita.

Dr. Chua decided that might be enough to convince the authorities to look into the leads provided by the apparent ghost of Teresita. He told them the whole story: Teresita was visiting his wife, and telling him that her murderer had stolen a pearl ring and a jade pendant from her, and that his name was Allan Showery. The Chuas didn't know it yet, but that name lined up with what the authorities had found at Teresita's apartment: the note saying to get tickets for A.S.

The detectives were baffled by the information but eventually agreed to follow up on the tip because the case had otherwise dried up, and they needed something to reignite the investigation.

Allan Showery was another respiratory therapist who worked with Teresita, Dr. Chua, and Remy Chua at Edgewater Hospital.

Stachula and Epplen visited Showery's home where he was

living with his girlfriend, Yanka Kalmuk. Showery went with the detectives freely and answered all their questions. Police had spoken to him earlier in their investigation, as they had already conducted interviews with everyone who worked with or knew Teresita. Detectives became suspicious of Showery when he seemed to change his original story and contradict little details.

Some accounts report that Showery claimed Teresita asked him to come over and fix her TV. He was allegedly having money troubles and Teresita wanted to help him out by giving him odd jobs. One story says he told officers he was planning to go and fix her TV, but she called and said she didn't need him to do it anymore. Another account says he went to fix the TV but either didn't have the parts, or didn't know how to do it, and promised he would come back later to finish the job.

One source even says that Kalmuk told police that he would have no idea how to fix a TV, as he had no technical skills. When the authorities spoke to her about the jewelry, she presented the exact pearl ring and a jade pendant that Teresita's voice had spoken of, saying Showery had given them to her as a 'late Christmas present.'

While in custody, Showery almost immediately confessed to police that he had killed Teresita.

Showery's lawyer, William Swano, called for the charges to be dropped, as he believed prosecutors didn't have probable cause to even look into Showery. He said, 'Never to my knowledge has a man been arrested because of a supernatural vision. Police have never before been informed of a criminal's

32

name from the grave.' He claimed that the whole interrogation and arrest were illegal without probable cause.

In response, a spokesperson for the prosecution said, 'It's not like we're going to cross-examine the voice ... We're really not interested in the supernatural aspect of this trial. The voice was an initial tip, but the evidence developed independently.'

Essentially, it didn't matter where the tip had come from. The authorities had a duty to investigate a lead which, as strange as it was, turned out to yield significant results, and result in a confession by the killer. Following up on a lead, no matter how weird, was not against procedure.

Besides, Showery had already been questioned as a suspect, as he worked with Teresita at the hospital. It wasn't as though the voice was implicating a completely random person who wasn't already part of the investigation. And Showery had freely gone to the station with police that day to answer questions.

A trial went ahead, but the jury was deadlocked, causing a mistrial.

While Showery was awaiting his second trial, he ended up taking a plea deal for a reduced sentence. The prosecution wanted to avoid another hung jury, while Showery wanted to avoid the possibility of a longer sentence if he went to trial and was found guilty.

Showery only served approximately six years in prison and was released in 1983. Some believe Teresita's ghost visited him in jail and influenced him to plead guilty. Following his release, he apparently lived a quiet, crime-free life.

Michael Malloy,
The Man Who Wouldn't Die

The U.S.A. was in the throes of Prohibition from 1920–1933. No alcohol was allowed to be sold, or consumed, but that didn't stop some from either selling or drinking it. It was the golden age of speakeasies: underground bars that allowed unsavory characters to congregate, selling questionable liquor.

They were also hard times financially. With the Great Depression raging, and liquor sales being illegal, times were hard for speakeasy owners like Tony Marino. People would come in, drink, and have no cash to pay with—and he obviously couldn't go to the police. He could barely afford his rent and was looking for a way to make some funds. Luckily, his bar was the meeting place for other seedy men looking for quick cash.

One night in July 1932, Marino, undertaker Francis

Pasqua, and grocer Daniel Kriesberg were in bad spirits while enjoying some illegal ones at Marino's bar. Marino confided in his drinking buddies that 'business is bad.'

Pasqua, a career criminal, let the table in on a scam he'd pulled the year before. He said he'd 'befriended' an alcoholic homeless woman, Mabelle Carlson, convinced her to declare him as a beneficiary on a $2,000 life insurance policy (almost $44,000 today), then set about killing her. He'd got her very drunk, drenched her and her mattress in water, then set her and her bed underneath an open window. The examiner found she'd died of bronchial pneumonia and Pasqua had walked away with a small fortune, no questions asked.

Pasqua suggested they pull the same scheme on a local drunk who frequented Marino's place, Michael Malloy. Michael had immigrated from Ireland. He was a homeless alcoholic who had no known family or friends, nor a steady job. He picked up gig work as a street cleaner but was more than happy to accept whiskey as payment. He was the perfect mark for an insurance scam.

Some sources say Pasqua got a friend to go with him to several insurance agencies to secure life insurance policies. The friend pretended to be a man called 'Nicholas Mellory,' and told the agents he declared his brother Joseph Murphy as his beneficiary.

In reality, Murphy was a bartender at Marino's bar who was being given a cut of the fraud to pretend that the dead Michael Malloy was 'Nicholas Mellory.' The plan was that the 'Murder Trust,' as the media eventually dubbed them, would kill Michael, then Joseph Murphy would tell the authorities he was his brother, Nicholas Mellory, and he would collect on the insurance policies.

It took five months of meetings, but the men eventually got three life insurance policies: one for $800 from the Metropolitan Life Insurance Company, and two each for $495 from Prudential Life Insurance Company. In the end, each man was to receive $3,576, which is the equivalent of around $54,000 today.

Other sources say Michael just drunkenly signed the policies himself, believing them to be petitions to let Marino run for local office. Either way, the men had secured the policies.

In December 1932, the Murder Trust set out to kill Michael Malloy. They assumed it would be an easy job. Michael was such a heavy drinker, they just assumed they could give him an open tab and he would drink himself to death. He would either succumb to alcohol poisoning, choke on his own vomit, or have an accident and die from his injuries.

They gave Michael an open tab, telling him that times were tough, so they had to ease the rules and offer free booze to compete with surrounding speakeasies. Michael took shot after shot, never wavering or tiring of drinking.

The open-tab plan continued for three days until the Murder Trust started to suspect that maybe Michael couldn't be taken out with simple alcohol. On day four, he allegedly burst into the bar saying 'Boy! Ain't I got a thirst!' and continued drinking.

The original three men recruited criminals John McNally,

Edward 'Tin Ear' Smith, 'Tough' Tony Bastone, and his associate Joseph Maglione to help them dispose of Michael.

'Tough' Tony suggested they just shoot him in the back of the head, but the rest of the men decided they needed the death to look more accidental to collect on the policy.

Bartender Joseph Murphy suggested they replace Michael's usual shots with wood alcohol and other poisonous substances. Wood alcohol is pure methanol. Only 4 per cent wood alcohol would make a person go blind, and since Prohibition, 50,000 people had died from overdoses of the substance, which they thought would work as well as alcohol.

Murphy started out giving Michael shots of his usual whiskey to get him 'feeling good,' before switching to wood alcohol. But he showed no signs of being affected by what was essentially poison. Some sources say the men also tried antifreeze, horse liniment, turpentine, and rat poison.

Michael continued coming into the bar for days, asking for shot after shot of one of the poisons the men were offering him. He didn't waver for days, until he stood and collapsed to the floor. His breath and pulse were both weak. The Murder Trust waited for Michael to pass away. They heard a sharp intake of breath they assumed to be his last, but then he started snoring. He had simply fallen asleep!

The men had noticed that Michael was a fan of seafood and thought if they soaked oysters in denatured alcohol and served it to him, he would experience serious gastrointestinal issues that would kill him. Instead, he ate the oysters and washed them down with wood alcohol, seeming to enjoy every bite.

In the same vein, they tried to feed him a sandwich of rotten sardines, mixed with shards of metal and tacks. Michael ate the sandwich, again with his glass of poison, and asked for another.

With the number of people the original planners had to cut in, plus the alcohol costs, and the monthly fees for the three life insurance policies, the plan was getting way too expensive.

The Trust decided to do what Pasqua had done to Mabelle Carlson and freeze Michael to death. After getting him drunk on the various poisons they had already tried, they drove him from Marino's place to Crotona Park, took his shirt off, and doused his head and torso in water, before leaving him for dead in the New York winter.

The next day, Marino went back to his bar and found Michael in the basement dressed in a new outfit and complaining of a 'wee chill.' Apparently, law enforcement had come by moments after the men had left him there and had taken him to a shelter where they gave him dry clothes.

The Trust then brought in yet another conspirator, cab driver Harry Green, who they promised $150 of the insurance cut if he would run Michael over with his taxi. Once again, the men got Michael drunk and took him for a ride. Two of the Trust propped him up while Harry sped at them. The two sober men were meant to jump out of the way and let Harry hit and kill the drunken Michael. He ended up also dodging the cab twice. On the third attempt, he was actually hit, and the men fled the scene, assuming he was finally dead.

Joseph Murphy, the bartender meant to be the 'brother' of the deceased man the Murder Trust had taken out a policy on, called around to hospitals and morgues 'looking' for his brother. There was no information on a fatal car accident.

Five days after they had run over Michael, with no information about where he'd gone, the men were looking into finding another homeless man to pass off as Nicholas Mellory so they could collect their insurance payouts.

Before they could finalize that plan, Michael Malloy walked through the door, saying, 'I sure am dying for a drink.'

Michael had very few memories of the night and certainly didn't know that the men were trying to kill him. He had simply woken up in Fordham Hospital and desperately wanted to get back to the bar.

On February 21, 1933, seven months after the seemingly simple plan had been hatched, the Murder Trust had had enough of waiting. They rented a room in a nearby tenement with gas lighting and, after getting Michael drunk again, they affixed a rubber tube from the gas fixture to his mouth, and gassed him to death.

A corrupt doctor friend of Pasqua's, Dr. Frank Manzella, created a fake death certificate, claiming the man died of lobar pneumonia.

The men collected the $800 policy from Metropolitan Life Insurance Company but couldn't get the two policies from Prudential. They needed to produce a body for Prudential to sign off. Pasqua said they'd already buried the body. Some sources say investigators went looking for Murphy, who claimed to be the deceased's brother, and found it suspicious that he was in jail at the time.

Michael Malloy's incredible tale was circulating the city, and eventually, cab driver Harry Green and the corrupt Dr. Manzella confessed to their part in the crime.

In May 1933, Michael was exhumed from his resting place in a pauper's field in Westchester County's Ferncliff Cemetery. His cause of death was confirmed, and Pasqua, Marino, Kriesberg, and Murphy were all convicted of first-degree murder and put to death by electric chair at Sing Sing prison.

Issei Sagawa, The Celebrity Cannibal

Imagine the worst crime you can think of. Now imagine that the person who committed it not only walked free but also became a celebrity because of it. This was the horrific reality faced by Renée Hartevelt's family after her gruesome death in 1981.

Issei Sagawa was born in Kobe, Japan, on April 26, 1949, to a wealthy family. A frail child, he later claimed to be 'weak from the moment [he] was born.' His divergent tendencies began at an extremely early age. He was interested in the cannibalistic story of *Hansel and Gretel* (sound familiar?), admitted to acts of bestiality with the family dog, and thought about biting into his classmates' thighs when he was just five years old.

Sagawa began obsessing over tall, white, Western women, like Grace Kelly, who became triggers for his cannibalistic urges. He said later that this urge stemmed from his insecurities, calling himself 'short and ugly.' Indeed, Sagawa was only five feet tall as an adult and was far from conventionally handsome. However, he also stated that cannibalism was 'just a fetish' like any other, and didn't stem from any need to suppress his dark feelings about himself.

At twenty-four years old, while still living in Tokyo, Sagawa noticed a tall, Western-looking woman walking down the street. His desperation to consume her flesh overpowered him, and he followed her to her apartment, wanting to wait until she was asleep, break in, and take a chunk of her flesh to eat later. Because he was so small and weak, however, the German woman was able to easily overpower him and call the police when she awoke to find the frail figure in her bedroom.

Sagawa admitted to the police that he had intended to sexually assault the woman but never admitted to his true desire, to steal her flesh and eat it. Sagawa's wealthy family was able to pay off the woman to drop the charges, and Sagawa went free for the first, but unfortunately not the last, time.

In 1977, Sagawa moved to France to study for his PhD at the Sorbonne in Paris. He continued to be a strange, unsettling person and did not have many friends. Luckily for the Parisians, his cannibalistic tendencies were squashed for a while, as he found French women to be 'stuck-up' and too obsessed with looks for his liking. He also claimed that they were 'out of [his] league.' This didn't stop him from being creepy and menacing though.

Sagawa said he would hire sex workers to his apartment and point a gun at them when their backs were turned. He never acted on the urge to shoot them, though, as he had an overwhelming feeling that everything would fall apart for him if he ever pulled the trigger.

He soon met Renée Hartevelt, a twenty-five-year-old Dutch woman in his literature class. She was kind, warm, and extremely intelligent, speaking English, French, and German. She seemed to him to be the opposite of the French girls who never gave him the time of day. Sagawa became obsessed with her and hatched a plan to get closer to her. He told her he wanted to read German poets in their original language, and asked her to come over and tutor him in German. She was more than happy to do so.

The pair spent many tutoring sessions together. Each time, as he did with the sex workers, Sagawa would point the gun at Renée when she wasn't looking, and each time he would simply put it down and continue his German studies.

One day, his mindset shifted. Sagawa had a fever, but despite feeling ill, he still went to dinner with a colleague of his father who was in town on business. During the meal, he deliriously obsessed over the idea that he might get food poisoning. He knew that if he were sick, then Renée wouldn't come over the next day, and he wouldn't have even the opportunity to kill her. He said it was the idea of this opportunity being taken away from him that made him make up his mind once and for all to go through with killing Renée.

Sagawa didn't get food poisoning. The next night, Renée came over as planned. As she sat in the living room, Sagawa again pointed his gun at the back of her head, only this time he pulled the trigger. The gun jammed. He merely set it down, acted as if nothing had happened, and the two continued to spend an otherwise pleasant evening together.

Sagawa did not see the gun's malfunction as a sign he shouldn't harm Renée. In fact, it seemed to fill him with even more resolve to get the job done.

Two days later, on June 11, 1981, Renée went over to Sagawa's apartment again. He once again pointed the gun at her, but this time there were no problems. He shot her point blank in the back of the neck. He was initially shocked that he had done it. He said later, 'the moment the girl became a corpse I realized I had lost an important friend, and even regretted killing her for a moment.'

He briefly considered calling an ambulance, but his cannibalistic urges took over, and he remembered why he had killed her in the first place. He told himself, 'Hang on, don't be stupid. You've been dreaming about this for thirty-two years and now it's actually happening.' His fleeting moment of regret passed as quickly as it had come on. Sagawa raped Renée's lifeless body, then began eating chunks of her flesh. Some of it he cooked, but most of it he ate raw.

He gorged himself on her body for the next two days. He later spoke incredibly candidly and disrespectfully of the process, even complaining about the flavor of certain parts of her body. He said the soles of her feet tasted the worst, and he enjoyed the tongue the most. Basically, he reported that the body tastes better as you move from the feet, upward. Sagawa also noted that Renée was on her period at the time, so her genitals did not taste very good, but he ate them anyway; he just did it quickly.

Once decomposition began to set in, Sagawa realized he had to dispose of what was left of the body. He removed some more chunks of her flesh and froze it to eat later, then dismembered the rest of her, and put the parts in two large suitcases. Sagawa hailed a cab to Bois de Boulogne Park and planned to dump the suitcases in a pond. A couple on a run in the park saw Sagawa and thought he was acting suspiciously. Some sources say they immediately called the police, while some say they looked in the suitcases after Sagawa left and saw the dismembered body of Renée.

The authorities were able to track down the cab driver who dropped Sagawa off at the park earlier that day, and the driver led them to the apartment where he was picked up. Police walked into a horrific scene and arrested Sagawa.

He was sent to a psychiatric facility. While awaiting the verdict from a judge, Sagawa wrote a graphic novel that described his crime in detail. He claimed it wasn't actually about what he had done, but it was about a man with canni-balistic urges who killed and ate a woman. The novel became popular and made Sagawa somewhat of a celebrity.

After two years in the facility, a judge decided that Sagawa was too insane to stand trial, so the charges were dropped. As Sagawa was in France on a student visa and wasn't a citizen of the country, he eventually needed to be deported back to Japan.

Sagawa was put into Tokyo's Matsuzawa Hospital, another psychiatric facility. The doctors on staff there, however, concluded that Sagawa was perfectly sane. Nothing could be done at that point to keep him off the streets. Since he had not been charged with a crime in Japan, and the case files in France were closed, Japanese authorities had no choice but to let Sagawa go. They couldn't keep a sane man in a psychiatric facility. On August 12, 1986, Sagawa left the hospital and was allowed to live a normal life in Japan.

Sagawa rode the wave of his celebrity and capitalized on his crime. He wrote dozens more books, gave tell-all interviews, and even allegedly made a cameo in a soft-core pornography movie.

In one of his tell-all interviews, with *Vice*, he was asked if he still had the urge to eat people. He said, 'Oh yes, definitely. The desire to eat people becomes so intense around June, when women start wearing less, and showing more skin ... There's no doubt in my mind that I want to eat human flesh again ... I mean, it's delicious stuff.' He noted that his obsession with tall, Western, blonde women had waned a little, and he was now interested in tasting a Japanese woman.

Sagawa also said he wished he was in jail or had been executed, not because he felt so bad about his crime, or was worried he would do it again, but because having to make his own way in society, make money, and find places to live is 'brutal.' He also complained about his celebrity, saying, 'You can't imagine how difficult it is to live under such constant surveillance from society.'

Sagawa died of pneumonia at the age of seventy-three, on November 24, 2022. As far as anyone knows, he did not fulfill his wish to taste more flesh before he died.

Daniel LaPlante,
The Ghost in the Walls

In 1986, in the small Massachusetts town of Pepperell, fifteen-year-old Tina Bowen and her nine-year-old sister Karen gathered around a Ouija board. The two young girls tried to contact their mother, who had died the year before from cancer. The girls got nothing from the Ouija session, but it still started a chain of events that would change their lives forever and lead to three exceedingly horrific deaths.

The night of their seance, the girls heard knocking on their walls while they tried to sleep. Thinking maybe contacting the spirits had worked, and their mother was trying to communicate with them, they asked the entity questions and got replies in more knocks and scratches on the walls. Had the girls actually managed to bring a spirit into their home?

Over the next few weeks, the knocking got more aggressive

and frequent. It began to disturb their sleep and deeply upset them. Their father, Frank, assumed the girls were just stressed from grief and were hearing things. However, the unexplainable haunting soon became more intrusive: unattended beverages would disappear from drinking glasses, objects moved around the home, and the TV would change channels on its own. Even furniture would be moved from one side of the room to the other.

The knocking continued to get stronger. It started in the girls' rooms, but eventually made its way all over the house. One day, while the girls were sitting in the living room, they heard the knocking coming from underneath them. Terrified, but needing answers, they took a kitchen knife and descended the stairs to the cellar. There, they found a note written in red on the wall saying 'I'm in your room. Come and find me.'

Frank continued to be a skeptic. He assumed one of them had written the note on the wall, acting out because of extreme grief. He sent the girls to counseling.

On December 8, 1986, the family returned home from an outing with the girls' friend Karen. They noticed that the toilet had been used but not flushed while they were gone. Frank went around the house investigating. He went into his room and noticed something off about his wardrobe. When he opened it, he was met with a crazed figure crouching down, wearing a 'hairy jacket.' His face was painted, his hair was greasy and unkempt, and he was carrying a hatchet in one hand and a wrench in the other.

Some sources have said the intruder was dressed in a wig

and an old dress of Frank's deceased wife, but while that does make for a sensational story, it is not true.

The figure calmly ordered the three girls and Frank into the bedroom where he menaced them with his weapons. Luckily, Tina was able to get away. She ran to their next-door neighbor's house and called the police.

The man had disappeared by the time the authorities arrived. The family was shaken up and very unsettled as it sank in that perhaps the disturbances they had been experiencing for the better part of a year had not been a ghost, but a person living in their walls, intentionally psychologically torturing them.

The Bowens stayed somewhere else while police investigated, understandably too scared to go back to the house while the culprit had not been found. Two days after the incident, Frank returned to the house to pick up a few things for the girls. As he approached the home, he noticed movement in the front window. He looked closer and saw the face of the man staring back at him.

Frank called the police and told them the man was still in their home. When the authorities arrived, they searched the home but couldn't find a person anywhere. What they did find were two family pictures that had been stabbed with kitchen knives, and two horrifying messages written on the walls. One said, 'I'm still here, come find me,' while the other plainly stated, 'I am going to kill you.'

But where had the perpetrator gone? Obviously, he had been living in the home for a while before taking the family hostage, and Frank had just seen him in the front window. The authorities didn't see any footprints in the snow leading away from the home. He had to be hiding somewhere that the police hadn't yet searched.

Eventually, the police found a tiny triangular crawlspace in the bathroom wall that housed the plumbing. To get to it, you would have to hoist yourself up over a four-foot foundation wall, squeeze through an eight-to-nine-inch-wide opening, and drop down into the space. It provided just enough room for someone to crouch down. The space also connected to the cellar, a floor below. An officer wriggled in and, gun drawn, jumped down. He saw nothing but what he thought was a pile of clothes, until he realized it was, in fact, hiding a person.

Officer Stephen Bezanson noted how eerily calm the intruder was, even when he threatened to shoot him. He said, 'He wasn't afraid to have a gun stuck next to his head.'

The person who had been terrorizing the Bowens was arrested and taken into custody, where it was discovered that he was someone who had once been on a date with Tina, Daniel LaPlante.

Daniel LaPlante was born on May 15, 1970 in Townsend, Massachusetts. According to Daniel, he endured horrific physical and sexual abuse at the hands of his father for most of his childhood. He acted out in school and didn't have many friends. He was sent to a psychiatrist and diagnosed with a hyperactive disorder. Daniel claimed his doctor also sexually abused him.

By the time he was fifteen, Daniel was already a seasoned

home invader and burglar. He didn't only want to steal things, though—he also wanted to terrorize the people living in the houses he broke into. He enjoyed playing mind games and would move objects around or leave items behind so the owners would know someone had been inside.

There are two different stories about how Tina and Daniel met. One says that in 1986 Daniel somehow got his hands on the Bowens' phone number. Some say he had broken into their house previously and managed to collect it, but this is unconfirmed. Either way, he began calling the house, telling Tina that he had gotten her number from a friend at her school, and he thought she was really pretty. He described himself as blond, tall, and athletic, the total opposite of what he actually looked like.

The two struck up a friendship, and eventually, Tina agreed to a date with him. When he showed up at the door she realized that he was not as he had described himself. She was unsettled by the lie and by Daniel's disheveled, greasy appearance. Tina agreed to go to a fair with him anyway, but it just got worse. Tina confided in Daniel that her mother had recently passed. Instead of having sympathy for her, he asked for details about how much her mother had suffered, and how she'd felt when she found out she had died. Tina made an excuse to leave about an hour into the date.

Tina was not at all interested in seeing Daniel again. The rejection seemed to make him even more obsessed with her, and he proceeded to move into her family home for the better part of a year.

The other story doesn't explain how the two met, but says that they went on one date, before Tina's friends informed her that Daniel was facing rape allegations, and she should probably stay away from him. Regardless of how things went down, the two had a very brief dalliance, and Tina was not interested in pursuing things further.

Once officers found Daniel in the family home, he was arrested and taken to a juvenile detention center where he stayed until October 1987. He was then sent to an adult facility, where his mother was able to post his $10,000 bail. He was released to his mother and stepfather's custody, to await his trial on December 11.

Almost immediately after being released, Daniel started breaking into houses again. He burglarized a home that was just a quarter mile from his mother's house, in broad daylight, on October 14, stealing cash and two guns.

Daniel's family started noticing that he had a lot of cash for someone who didn't have a job and was supposed to just be staying at home awaiting a trial. His mother found one of the guns he had stolen, and he lied and said he had had it before he was even arrested.

On November 16, 1987, Daniel broke into the Gustafson house, which was just through the woods to the back of his own house. He took a cordless phone, cable boxes, and the remotes that went with them. What he intended to do with these items is unknown. Could he have been planning another 'haunting'?

Reports say that Daniel asked his brother and his brother's

friend for bullets that would fit the gun he stole. He somehow convinced them that he just wanted to perform an experiment where he melted the bullets down and reformed the metal into something else. It's uncertain whether the brother actually believed this, considering Daniel's strange criminal past, but he gave him the bullets anyway.

On December 1, 1987, Daniel once again broke into the Gustafson house. He claimed he was not expecting anyone to be home to interrupt his usual trawling around and moving items to scare the occupants. However, nursery-school teacher Priscilla Gustafson and her five-year-old son William came home while Daniel was in the house.

He shoved William in a closet, made makeshift restraints from stockings and other clothing, tied Priscilla up, raped her, placed a pillow to her head, and shot her.

Daniel then took William to the bathroom and drowned him in the tub. Seven-year-old Abigail Gustafson then came home from school, and Daniel drowned her in the family's other bathroom.

He then left the home and attended his niece's birthday party.

Andrew Gustafson came home to an eerily quiet house. Normally his two young children would be running around, playing, and making noise, but they were nowhere to be seen or heard. He walked into his bedroom to find his wife tied up and shot. He immediately called the police, but said he was too afraid to look for his children, as their continued silence was not a good sign.

The authorities found footprints matching a size 11/12 Converse shoe in the flower beds outside the home, and saw that a few items were missing, including the metal 'Gustafson' nameplate from the front of the house.

Police dogs tracked a scent to the woods between the Gustafson home and Daniel's mother's house. On December 2, police found the nameplate in the woods, along with a flannel shirt and a pair of work gloves that later turned out to have gunshot residue on them.

The police dogs led officers right to Daniel's home, but not before Daniel fled. A search of the home found the rest of the items that had been stolen from the Gustafson's and the gun used to kill Priscilla. A manhunt ensued.

Daniel spent the next day desperately breaking into houses looking for supplies so he could stay hidden for as long as possible. However, the search didn't last long. Police found Daniel hiding in a dumpster on December 3.

In 1988, Daniel was found guilty of three counts of murder and was sentenced to three life sentences.

In 2017, Daniel appealed for a reduced sentence, but the judge said he was clearly not regretful of his hideous crimes and upheld the three life sentences. Daniel will not even potentially be eligible for parole until he has served forty-five years.

The Miyazawa Murders

Kamisoshigaya Street in the Setagaya neighborhood of Tokyo, Japan, used to be a bustling area with more than two hundred homes and businesses. By 2000, though, only four of those houses were occupied. The city was planning on using the space to expand Soshigaya Park and had already given most of the residents a large sum of money as a relocation bonus.

Two of the four remaining houses belonged to the same family. In one lived Miyazawa Mikio, a forty-four-year-old man, his wife, forty-one-year-old tutor Yasuko, and their two children—eight-year-old Niina and six-year-old Rei. Right next door lived Yasuko's sister, An; her husband; and Yasuko and An's mother, Haruko.

On December 30, 2000, Niina spent the afternoon at her aunt and grandmother's home, watching a video on their computer. It was the last time they would see her alive. The

Miyazawa family had a normal evening at home together. At some point, Rei was put to bed in the second-floor bedroom, Mikio was working on the first floor, while Yasuko and Niina cuddled up on a futon in the third-floor attic, possibly sleeping.

The authorities believe that around 11:30 p.m., a man climbed up a tree to the second-floor bathroom, removed the screen from the window, and entered the home. The man first went to the next room, where six-year-old Rei was sleeping. It seems the intruder paced around the room for a while, or perhaps kept returning to the room, as this is where police found the most footprints. The man strangled the young boy and set about murdering the rest of the family.

Because there were no survivors and it was such a hectic, bloody scene, the authorities cannot be sure exactly what happened next. The best guess is that the intruder went downstairs to where Mikio was working. Mikio was either already on his way upstairs or confronted the man when he came down from the second floor. The intruder stabbed him with a sashimi knife he'd brought to the home. Mikio had stab wounds all over his body and part of the knife blade was found in the back of his skull.

It is then thought that the murderer went back upstairs and began attacking Yasuko and Niina in the attic, only to find that his knife was too broken to inflict the damage he intended. He probably went back downstairs to the kitchen to get another knife, seeing as the second murder weapon found in the home belonged to the Miyazawas' own knife set.

It is thought that while the murderer had temporarily left the two alone, Yasuko may have carried Niina down to the second floor and attempted to dress her wounds with the family's first aid kit. Niina's blood was found on the kit, as well as in the attic, so this timeline lines up with the evidence. The murderer came back up the stairs to where the desperate mother was trying to save her daughter's life and brutally stabbed both Yasuko and Niina to death. The two were found crouched back-to-back.

The next morning, Haruko called the home to speak to her daughter. There was no answer. She found this odd, as it was not only a Sunday, but also New Year's Eve, so the family should definitely have been home. She called several more times, never getting an answer. Feeling uneasy, she decided to go next door to check on them. Knocking at the door was also met with no answer.

She remembers using her spare key to get into the home and finding the horrific scene that lay within. She saw Mikio first, stabbed multiple times, lying in his own blood by the foot of the stairs. Panicked, Haruko ran up the stairs in search of her daughter and grandchildren. On the second floor, her worst fears were confirmed. She found Yasuko and Niina, stabbed and covered in blood in the hallway, and Rei lying lifeless in his bed.

Police were called at 10:56 a.m., and one of the most bizarre investigations in the country's history began.

The perpetrator had left behind heaps of evidence that should have immediately led to an identification and a speedy arrest. In the bathroom, they found a desk drawer from the first floor that had been dumped out into a full bathtub. Yasuko's belongings from her purse, as well as Mikio's wallet and keys, were also found in the tub. But that's not the strange part. After all, home invaders ransack houses all the time.

The weird thing wasn't what he did with the Miyazawas' belongings, but what he left behind of his own.

In the bathroom, the authorities found a blood-soaked towel, and sanitary pads the murderer had used in an attempt to dress his own wounds. He had used the bathroom but hadn't flushed the toilet. His fingerprints were all over the home, and on the murder weapons, which were both left on the second floor beside Yasuko and Niina's bodies. Police found four empty ice cream packets on which they found the killer's saliva. He had also left behind essentially an entire outfit: a bucket hat, a long-sleeved baseball-style shirt, a jacket, a scarf, two handkerchiefs, a pair of shoes, gloves, and a belt bag. On the bag, they also found the perpetrator's hair. The authorities had this person's fingerprints, hair, saliva, blood, and even feces.

Police assumed it would be an open and shut case once they ran everything through their databases. Japan has an extensive DNA database, as everyone who has ever committed a crime, and even those who have merely been suspected of a crime, are compelled to give a DNA sample to the government. With a crime as brutal as this one, police assumed the perpetrator must already be in the system, having committed or been suspected of a smaller crime in the past. People don't just suddenly start a life of crime by murdering an entire family, including two young children, in their fairly secluded home. However, nothing came up in the databases.

Five million people from Tokyo and the surrounding area had their fingerprints tested, and still, nothing was a match. The blood was found to be male and type A, which was different from all the Miyazawas' blood types, making the authorities sure it was the killer's. However, without a match to anyone in the system, knowing the blood type was next to useless.

The authorities set about investigating every piece of clothing the perpetrator had left behind. They found that the hat was only sold from September 1999 to November 2000, the gloves from 1998–2000, and the jacket was a 2000 release from Uniqlo. Since the crimes happened at the end of 2000, these dates seemed to suggest that the killer had bought everything near the date of the crime. Perhaps he bought them especially to leave behind at the scene, to throw police off his trail, and they didn't necessarily come directly from his closet. Because so many units of each of these items were sold in stores all across the country, their identification didn't help the investigation much.

The scarf did seem to have a lot more wear and tear to it, suggesting it may have belonged to the killer for some time. Police found that this style of scarf, made of plaid wool, was popular with young and college-aged people at the time. It had also been given away as a promotion at many stores throughout the city, so it was impossible to track down everyone who had ever owned one, although it did make the police suspect that the killer was on the younger side.

The shirt, the belt bag, the handkerchiefs, and the shoes the perpetrator had left behind provided some more clues as to the killer's origins, but left investigators even more baffled than before.

Around three hundred of that same shirt had been purchased in all of Japan. However, it was only available in four stores in Tokyo, and only ten had ever been sold from those four stores. The killer could have been one of just ten people, but police were unable to track them all down.

The belt bag had adjustable straps that had been pulled tight, suggesting the killer had a slim build. Inside, police found sand that the lab concluded had come from the southwest of the United States. Some sources say it came from a specific air force base, leading some to believe the killer had been in the military, or been the child of a military family that was stationed in Japan at the time.

One of the two handkerchiefs found in the bathroom had a deliberate slit in the middle of it, leading investigators to believe that the killer had used it to protect the handle of his knife. Police noted it was a technique used by Chinese fish-factory workers to make sure their knives don't get wet and slippery as they gut the fish. Both handkerchiefs also smelled like Drakkar Noir cologne, which was apparently a scent popular with skateboarders in the country in the eighties. Police found this interesting, as the Miyazawas' home backed on to a skate park, and witnesses said Mikio was often seen arguing with the skaters, who made a lot of noise and were generally disrespectful. Again, nothing came from that lead.

The shoes became one of the most interesting pieces of evidence. They were Slazenger, a brand produced in South Korea and sold in both Korea and Japan. However, the size of this particular pair of shoes was only sold in South Korea. Soil from the soles of the shoes was also traced to South Korea.

The case remained unsolved and mystifying for years, till in 2005, a DNA expert was able to create a genetic profile for the killer. They found that the killer had East Asian roots on his father's side (Japanese, Chinese, or Korean), that his mother was of Eastern European descent, and his maternal grandparents were from the Mediterranean part of Eastern Europe. Some sources even narrowed it down to countries bordering the Adriatic Sea, like Croatia, Montenegro, or Albania.

He also had a genetic marker that showed up in one in thirteen Japanese people, one in ten Chinese people, and one in five Koreans, making it even more likely the killer hailed from South Korea.

With the shoe evidence, and the genetic marker leading the authorities to believe the man was Korean, they reached out to the country for help, but the government denied Japanese authorities access to their databases.

Some believe police fumbled the case by not looking into various leads that popped up right after the murders. Suspects or suspicious people may have been overlooked because police were looking for a person with certain injuries, despite not knowing exactly where the killer's injury was. It was assumed to be on one of his arms or hands from the bloody blade slipping, but it could have been somewhere else.

Even so, one woman said that on the night in question, a man with an injured hand darted out in front of her car near the neighborhood, and police never followed up that lead either. In an article on the anniversary of the crime, police encouraged that woman to reach out again and give an official statement.

Over the years, more than 240,000 police officers have worked on the case, with some investigating it full time. The chief of police from the time of crime has since retired but continues to investigate it unofficially. As of 2020, there have been 13,000 tips from the public, but nothing has ever moved investigators close to even naming a suspect.

Kevin Ives and Don Henry,
The Boys on the Tracks

On August 23, 1987, at about 4 a.m., train engineer Stephen Shroyer was on his regular route through Saline County, Arkansas. When the seventy-five-car freight train reached the outskirts of Bryant, Arkansas, he saw something that would change his life forever.

Stephen noticed two figures on the tracks, partially covered by a light-green tarp. He was alarmed but expected the figures to move out of the way, or at least to look up. The engineer began the braking process for the train, but a 6,000-ton train traveling at fifty miles per hour can't just stop on a dime. A half-mile later, the train finally came to a stop, but not before it had run over the lifeless bodies laid across the tracks.

Shroyer and his colleagues called the authorities, noting

that there was a .22 rifle and a flashlight on the gravel near the bodies.

At about 5 a.m., Linda Ives, a Bryant resident, got a call from family friend Curtis Henry asking if she knew where their sons were. Linda was a little perturbed by the question, considering her son, Kevin, was supposed to be spending the night at the Henry house with Curtis's son, Don.

Curtis informed Linda that the boys had left the house at around 12:15 a.m., planning to go 'spotlighting', an illegal form of hunting where you shine a flashlight in the eyes of an animal to stun it and make it easier to shoot. The boys were also going to meet up with several friends throughout the night: some who wanted to come hunting with them and a few they'd meet up with in a grocery store parking lot to hang out and smoke pot.

Curtis called Linda back a little later that morning with the horrific news that their sons had been shot, tied to the train tracks, and run over. That information turned out to be a little exaggerated, based on gossip from the townspeople who turned up to witness the initial investigation after the train accident. The figures on the tracks had not been shot, nor tied to the tracks. What the rumor got right, though, was that the figures on the tracks were seventeen-year-old Kevin Ives and sixteen-year-old Don Henry.

Arkansas medical examiner Dr. Fahmy Malak came to a questionable conclusion. His statement said: 'At 4:25 a.m. on August 23, 1987, Larry Kevin Ives (17), and Don George Henry (16) were unconscious and in a deep sleep on the railroad tracks under the psychedelic influence of THC (marijuana), when a train passed over them, causing their accidental death.'

Malak insisted the boys were still alive when the train hit them, and that they had the equivalent of '20 joints' of marijuana in their systems. He suggested that the boys possibly smoked a lot to knock themselves out, and then voluntarily lay on the tracks to commit suicide.

The boys' parents were very suspicious of this conclusion. Neither boy had seemed depressed, nor had they been experiencing any mental health issues. The parents set about getting a second opinion. According to Linda Ives, they attempted to get the samples collected from the scene sent to a different lab. She recalls that they were met with a lot of resistance, but eventually the samples were sent to Dr. J. T. Francisco in Memphis, Tennessee.

The boys' parents were very disappointed to learn that Dr. Francisco had come to the same conclusion as Dr. Malak. Linda looked through all the lab reports with a fine-tooth comb and realized that Dr. Francisco hadn't even been sent a sample of Don's urine, only Kevin's, and yet, had come to the conclusion that Don had also had high levels of THC in his system.

The parents kept questioning Francisco until he admitted he'd just agreed with Malak's opinion without actually testing any of the samples he was given. He said Malak had enough experience and expertise that he assumed the tests had been done correctly in the first place.

The Iveses and Henrys held a press conference to put pressure on the authorities to continue to look into the case, believing that the official report was completely untrue.

Deputy Prosecutor Richard Garrett contacted the family and wanted to take on their case. He said he agreed that it was highly unlikely that the boys had committed suicide.

On February 18, 1988, a prosecutor's hearing began. Forty experts, EMTs, and bystanders from the scene testified. Paramedics from the scene said the boys' blood was way too dark and deoxygenated to have been fresh, suggesting that they had been dead before they were hit by the train. A friend of the boys who had briefly joined them on their hunting trip said they smoked one or two joints between them—certainly nowhere near twenty.

It was noted that the light-green tarp the people on the train saw covering the boys was never admitted into evidence. The authorities said the tarp never actually existed, and they were experiencing an optical illusion.

With so much weird evidence coming up, the families decided that they wanted second autopsies done on the boys. Their bodies were exhumed and Georgia medical examiner Dr. Joseph Burton performed new autopsies. What he found in his autopsies was shockingly contradictory to Dr. Malak's initial reports.

The THC in their systems was consistent with the version of events their friend had given. Maybe one or two joints had been shared between the boys, but not twenty. Dr. Burton also found a wound on Don's back and a tear in his shirt that were consistent with a stabbing. Further, he detected an injury on Kevin's face that appeared to have been caused by a blow from the butt of a rifle that, due to the swelling, had to have happened before he died.

Dr. Burton suggested the verdict in the case be changed to homicide.

But what had happened that night that warranted the murder of two young boys? Did they witness something they shouldn't have? Many believe that to be the case.

In the eighties, Arkansas had a big drug problem. Mena, Arkansas, a couple of hours' drive from Bryant, was known to be a hub for trafficking. Many people suggested that the boys stumbled upon a drug drop happening in the woods that night and were murdered.

Considering all the new evidence that was coming to light, a grand jury was called to review the case. It convened on April 27, 1988. Attorney Dan Harmon was assigned to lead the proceedings.

Many people were subpoenaed to give their testimony to the jury. Some were heard, but others mysteriously disappeared, died, or were murdered before they could tell the jury what they knew.

Keith Coney, a friend of the boys who had hung out with them in the parking lot the night they were murdered, died in a motorcycle crash. It was deemed an accident, but witnesses say he was being chased before the crash, and even that they thought his throat had been slashed. No autopsy was ordered.

James Milam, a witness to the Mena drug trade, who claimed he had information about the murders, was found decapitated in his home. Dr. Malak ruled his death to be due to complications from an ulcer and said that the family dog had eaten his head. The head was then found a few blocks away, in a trash can.

Greg Collins, another person claiming to have information about the murders, was found shot in the face in the woods. Malak ruled it a suicide.

Keith McKaskle claimed to be there at the tracks that night and that he knew exactly who had killed Kevin and Don. He was found in his driveway, stabbed 113 times.

Similar suspicious deaths befell potential grand jury witnesses Jeff Rhodes, Boonie Beardson, Richard Winters, Jordan Ketelsen, and Mike Samples.

Still, the grand jury went on and continued to uncover strange things. A very similar death had occurred in 1984, in an Oklahoma town just 150 miles away from Bryant. Twenty-one-year-old Billy Hainline and twenty-six-year-old Dennis Decker were also killed on train tracks, lying side by side, not even looking up while the train barreled toward them. The case was never investigated as a homicide.

As the grand jury proceeded, Linda Ives became very suspicious of Dan Harmon. She alleged that he told her and Don Henry's family that he was having money troubles, and that both families would cut him a cheque for $500 every few weeks, though these accusations have not been confirmed by the authorities.

Rumors started circulating around town that Harmon was actually in the drug scene himself.

A few days before the grand jury was set to disband, the *Arkansas Democrat* published Dr. Malak's various testimonies about the case, noting one major discrepancy: in May he had said that the boys' lungs were heavier than average because they had inhaled a lot of fluid, probably their own blood. In November, he said they were heavier than average because they had been weighed with other organs.

This change is significant because if the first one is correct, and they had inhaled blood, then the boys must have been injured *before* they were hit by the train. The change in testimony points toward Malak wanting to corroborate the story he came up with later.

Despite everything that had gone wrong in the case, and Malak's obviously suspicious moves, the Arkansas Sheriffs' Association said it backed Malak and all his findings, regardless of if they turned out to be false. Malak not only kept his job, but was given a raise and a larger office. The grand jury finished its inquest, but John Cole, the judge in the case, refused to release a report of its findings, ruling that because they had found that Bryant had a significant drug problem, the police should be following those leads and they ought not be made public.

The one good thing to come from the investigation is that the official causes of death were changed to homicide. However, the new leads uncovered by the jury were barely followed up on, and the case fell flat.

In March 1990, Deputy Prosecutor Jean Duffey was asked to head up a new drug task force. Her supervisor, Prosecuting Attorney Gary Arnold, told her she wasn't to use the task force to investigate public officials. As soon as her agents began investigating, however, they were able to link several public officials, including Dan Harmon, to drug activities. She reported the information to the U.S. Attorney's office anyway.

Articles began coming out accusing Jean of embezzlement, illegal arrests, and child endangerment. She was soon served a subpoena to appear at a hearing that would force her to reveal her sources. She ignored the subpoena and fled the state instead. A felony arrest warrant was issued, for what would normally be a misdemeanor. Jean said she thought she would be jailed if she showed up for the hearing, and feared for her life if she were put into an Arkansas jail after learning what she knew about the officials in the area. She was almost certain the 'smear campaign' and subpoena were the work of Dan Harmon, though, once again, authorities have not confirmed that Harmon had anything to do with them.

In 1992, an *L.A. Times* article came out detailing all of Dr. Malak's suspicious rulings, including saying a man who was shot in the chest five times had committed suicide. The public wanted him removed as the state medical examiner. Governor Bill Clinton refused to remove him from his office. Malak not only wasn't removed from office, but he was also, once again, given a massive raise.

A new detective, John Brown, was assigned to the boys'

case. He was told by higher-ups to leave it alone and not investigate any further. He didn't listen. He found the file to be lacking a ton of significant information, such as evidence lists. He began re-interviewing witnesses and examining statements.

By November 1996, Dan Harmon had become Saline County Prosecutor. He was driven out of office after he assaulted and kidnapped a reporter. Harmon was further looked into and more accusations against him started coming to light.

A grand jury was convened in April 1997, which eventually charged Harmon with racketeering, extortion, and distribution. The rumors were true: Dan Harmon was part of the Arkansas drug trade. Every case he had ever touched was suddenly considered to be tainted, including that of Kevin Ives and Don Henry.

In 2018, the case got slightly stranger. A former pro-wrestler, Billy Haynes, contacted Linda Ives saying he knew who had killed the boys. He said he had worked as 'muscle' for the Arkansas drug trade and had been asked by a 'criminal politician' to make sure all the money from a drug drop made it to where it was supposed to go. He said the boys were murdered by people working for the same 'criminal politician.'

Despite the corruption uncovered in relation to the majority of the important people in this case, no definitive verdict has ever been reached about the deaths of Kevin Ives and Don Henry.

Christina Kettlewell, The Eight-Day Bride

On May 20, 1947, the body of Christina Kettlewell was found just 150 feet from the Severn Falls cabin where she was spending her honeymoon with her husband John Ray Kettlewell, who went by Jack, and the couple's friend, Ronnie Barrie. She was dressed in floral pajamas, was barefoot, and had apparently drowned in only nine inches of water, while the rest of her body was on otherwise dry land.

Christina Mocon was born in Mimico, outside of Toronto, in Ontario, Canada. She worked at the Bank of Nova Scotia. Chris had been in an on-and-off relationship with Jack Kettlewell since she had met him at the age of sixteen. Jack's best friend, Ronnie, followed him everywhere he went. A friend of Chris recalls her saying she wasn't totally sure about pursuing the romance with Jack, as she knew she would get Ronnie as well, and 'nobody wants two husbands.'

While Jack was stationed overseas during the war, in the Royal Dental Corps, Ronnie looked after Chris, taking her out on dates just like Jack would. Chris's family assumed Ronnie was also in love with Chris, but she insisted they were just close friends.

Chris's family disapproved of her relationship with Jack. They were from a strict Polish Catholic background and didn't want Chris marrying someone who wasn't of their faith.

On May 12, 1947, the two eloped to avoid scrutiny from her family. After spending a few days at an apartment in Toronto, shopping and celebrating, they got in Ronnie's car, and he drove them to his five-room cottage in Severn Falls. Ronnie said he initially didn't plan on staying, but he thought Chris was acting distant and agitated, and worried that something bad might happen if he left the couple alone.

Ronnie was down by the water on the evening of May 20, 1947. There are two conflicting accounts of what happened when he returned to the cabin. One says he arrived to find the cabin on fire and went inside to find a delirious Jack, confused, apparently drugged, having suffered a head wound, with Christina nowhere to be found.

The other account says Christina was in the room at the time but wouldn't answer when Ronnie asked what had happened to Jack. He then picked up Jack and took him outside to treat his wounds, and then noticed the cabin was on fire. He said he went back to find Chris, but she was no longer there. Either way, Jack was injured, the cabin was on fire, and Christina had disappeared.

Major Lawrence Scardifield, a first responder to the fire, went down to the river to get buckets of water, and didn't see Chris's body in the spot where it was found hours later.

Jack and Ronnie had gone to the mainland to get Jack's wounds and burns looked at. Once he was released from the hospital, Jack was questioned by police for three hours. Ronnie, on the other hand, was questioned for a whopping thirteen hours and had produced a rambling three-thousand-word statement by the end of it.

An inquiry was launched to investigate the death and the potential arson of the cabin. Press coverage was massive, and Jack and Ronnie became unlikely celebrities, even signing autographs outside the courthouse.

Ronnie spun the same bizarre tale at the inquest that he had told the police. He said that Chris was suicidal, and even wanted to kill Jack if she couldn't have him. He produced three suicide notes allegedly written by Chris. The first was written on Easter Sunday, five weeks before the elopement. It was addressed to Ronnie and spoke of attempting to poison herself due to 'the uncertainty of receiving a proposal' from Jack. It continued, 'This will be the best way out, as I cannot bear to see another girl have him.'

The second note, also addressed to Ronnie, was allegedly found at Jack and Ron's apartment after he had walked in on Jack and Chris unconscious and unable to be roused. Ronnie said he was able to get both of them to vomit the poison up, and then the three of them went to the cabin for a week to recover.

The second letter read:

Dear Ronnie, I guess when you read this letter things will be kind of changed some. You stopped me from doing anything the last time but this time you won't know anything until it's all over. I hate to do this to you as I know the spot it will place you in, and the explanation that will have to be made. No kidding. I feel like a heel placing you in such a predicament as you've been better than a brother to me. But what can I do? When you love someone, you really love them, and I know there is no one for me but Jack, and if I can't have him, I don't want anyone else to. I have waited years you might say, in the hopes that Jack would ask me to marry him, but I now realize I am just a passing fancy where he is concerned, and as I've said to you many times, if I can't have him, no one else is going to have him. I just couldn't bear the thought of another girl being Mrs. Kettlewell. Jack is in the bedroom asleep, little knowing what is coming . . . I hope you won't judge me too harshly, but you know what I told you would happen if Jack threw me aside. Please say goodbye to Mrs. Thomas and the others for me. I guess there is not much more to say—Thanks for everything. I really wish things could have been different but such is life, I guess. Don't blame yourself for anything. It certainly isn't your fault that things didn't turn out. Thanks again, Chris

This note was suspicious for several reasons. It skewed heavily toward how good of a person Ronnie was, and that there should be no blame placed on him for the murder–suicide. It was odd that Chris asked Ronnie to say goodbye to their landlady (Mrs. Thomas), but essentially said nothing of her family or friends. Jack said he knew nothing of the notes, which is also strange, as you would think if his best friend's girlfriend was suicidal, and Jack's life was in danger as a result, Ronnie may have mentioned this to him.

It also mentioned several previous conversations Ronnie had allegedly had with Chris concerning suicidal tendencies and her wish to harm Jack if he didn't propose to her. According to Chris's sisters, she hadn't shown any sign that any of that was true. Chris and Jack had been on-and-off for years, and their periods apart never seemed to affect Chris as much as the letter had implied. Chris had even been engaged to a different man for a short period and certainly didn't seem to be particularly pining for Jack.

Chris's sisters also noted that Chris had shared a different memory of the time before the week-long stint at the cabin. She had confided in her sisters that she had woken several times, nude and disoriented, after eating something at Jack and Ronnie's apartment. She thought she was being drugged and possibly assaulted and was scared of the men. It was after one of these incidents that Ronnie and Jack had taken Chris to the cabin. Some think the men were performing what was known as *fuitina* in Italy, where a young girl and her beau run away together for a short while, to imply to the families and to the rest of the community that they had been sexually intimate. This would usually force the families to agree to a marriage they had previously disapproved of, seeing as the young girl would have been ruined in the eyes of society, and of God.

Indeed, just a few days after the trio returned from the cabin, Jack and Chris eloped.

Ronnie miraculously produced a third suicide note in which Chris apparently admits to having a hand in what would happen later that day. Ronnie said Chris had written it the afternoon of her death and had given it to him to send to Mrs. Thomas. This final note read: 'Ronnie is in the boat outside somewhere. By the time he gets back everything will be all over with. He must have been afraid something would happen because he is still staying an extra day, to make sure we go back to Toronto with him.'

Again, this note paints Ronnie as a caring person, explains why he was still at the cabin even though it was supposed to be his friend's honeymoon, and once again absolves him of any guilt or suspicion for whatever it is Chris is admitting to doing.

Crown Prosecutor C. P. Hope called Ronnie 'a liar of the most blatant kind, whose sinister figure permeates the whole of this tragedy, but whose purpose and design are shrouded in mystery.'

Ronnie's purpose, as it turns out, may have been insurance fraud. He had fallen on hard times financially. His businesses were failing, and he was taking loans from anyone who would give them to him.

Insurance policies of $5,000 each had been taken out on

both Jack and Chris's lives. They both involved a double indemnity clause, meaning the beneficiary would receive double the amount if the death was ruled accidental. That beneficiary happened to be Ronnie. Ronnie had also taken out new policies on his cabin to cover theft and arson. He then gave a statement saying he had lost $500 in the cabin fire, and Jack, another $200. In today's money, that would be over $11,000, which seems an excessive amount of cash for a man with several debts and failing businesses. Was Ronnie just trying to pad the insurance claim?

The evidence surrounding Chris's death being suspicious was also piling up. Helen, Chris's sister, said that Chris felt like she was being drugged frequently around the time of the marriage. She basically said Chris was unsure of what was going on and 'came to, married,' meaning she was essentially in a daze and, when she regained consciousness, she had already married Jack.

The police report stated a 'strong suspicion' that Chris's state of mind was something 'other than normal' before her death. The authorities suggested drugs or medication could be the reason, but were unable to confirm whether Chris took these substances voluntarily, or if she was drugged.

The codeine found in her system was the same kind that Jack and Ronnie's landlord, Richard Thomas, was prescribed. He testified that he kept his tablets in a nondescript box and that Chris probably wouldn't have known they were there, or what they were. He said Ronnie, on the other hand, had picked up his prescription for him in the past, so would know exactly what they were and what they looked like. Mr.

Thomas even said he was missing a few tablets around the time of Chris's death. Not only that, but he said Chris had told him that 'if Ronnie went on their honeymoon with them, something would happen.'

Chris's autopsy also found no signs of her walking barefoot through the woods. She had one cut on the top of one of her toes, but that was it. She had apparently drowned in the nine inches of water by the banks of the river, yet the rest of her body, including the back of her head, was dry. Was her body carried and dumped down by the river? Again, the first responder who arrived to help put out the fire said he didn't see her body where it was later found.

The inquiry's findings ended up being inconclusive as far as Christina's death was concerned. They were unable to say without a shadow of a doubt that her death was the result of foul play, though strangely they did say the fact that she had drowned was 'suspicious.'

No arrests were made, and Jack and Ronnie walked. Jack remarried three years later and started a family. Ronnie moved to the U.S.A. in 1956 and nobody, not even his closest confidant, Jack, ever heard from him again.

Jack's son Richard said that he and his wife stumbled across the story while doing genealogy research at the library. His father had never spoken of his first wife or the suspicious way that she had died. He said his father was always a reserved man, who wasn't a big talker and avoided confrontation. If he was involved in an insurance-fraud scheme, Richard is certain Jack was 'manipulated and dominated' by Ronnie.

Murder at the Red Barn

The murder of Maria Marten quickly became one of England's most sensational crimes. After all, as if murder wasn't enough, this case involves illicit affairs, psychic visions, bloodthirsty crowds, and a lingering curse.

Maria Marten was born in 1801 to a fairly poor family. Her father, Thomas, was a mole-catcher in the village of Polstead in Suffolk. He made his living by skinning moles and making their hides into gloves. After Maria's mother passed away, Thomas had re-married Ann, a woman only a few years older than his daughter.

Maria was a beautiful, bright young girl. One account says that a fortune teller once told her she would have many lovers and riches but would not reach old age. She turned out to be right about two of those three things.

In her early twenties, Maria began a love affair with a man named Thomas Corder, the son of a wealthy farm owner.

When she got pregnant, Thomas abandoned her. It didn't take long for Maria to replace him, and before she had the baby, she began a relationship with a man named Peter Matthews.

Maria's child with Corder died not long after it was born. When Maria became pregnant by Matthews, she once again discovered that the father-to-be was not interested in raising a child or being the subject of scandal for having a child out of wedlock. He promised to send Maria money, but refused to marry her or have any part in the child's life.

Soon after Maria gave birth, she met Thomas Corder's brother, William. William had a reputation as a thief and a petty criminal. After he tried to sell some of his father's livestock without permission, his father had sent him to London with a little money to try and find work, and make something out of himself. William wasted the money on his lascivious lifestyle and fell into a life of crime. When his father and brothers all fell ill, he had had to return to the farm to help his mother run it.

William's father passed away from tuberculosis, and his two brothers suffered permanent damage from the disease, which left them unable to work. Thomas, William's eldest brother, and the father of Maria's first baby, died soon after his father, falling through the ice into a freezing lake. His other brother also died tragically young, leaving William as the man of the house, and the owner of the family farm.

William began an affair with Maria. Understandably, her parents did not approve of the relationship, considering William's reputation, and the fact that his brother had abandoned her while she was pregnant with his child. William and Maria were forced to meet in secret. Their favorite spot for dalliances was the Red Barn, a landmark in the town.

After several sessions at the barn, Maria found out she was pregnant for the third time. William, unlike his brother, promised Maria and her family that he would marry her. Any doubts about the relationship had to be put aside. Maria was a poor, single mother, who had, by the standards of early nineteenth-century England, completely disgraced herself by having several children out of wedlock. William was a wealthy landowner and might have been the last opportunity for Maria to find a man who would marry her, and provide for her family.

William sent Maria away to Sudbury to have their baby, to avoid prying eyes. The infant died two weeks later and was clandestinely buried, again, to avoid the further damage to both of their reputations that a bastard child could bring. Some say that William had something to do with the child's death, as he never intended to marry Maria, though that cannot be definitively proven.

After this tragic incident, the couple's relationship became rockier. They fought all the time, and Maria suspected William was stealing the money Peter Matthews was sending her as child support. William promised he still intended to marry Maria but avoided making any concrete plans to do so.

Suddenly, William had a complete change of heart. He suggested he and Maria run away to Ipswich to elope in secret. He even told her there was a warrant out for her arrest for having illegitimate children. It's unclear whether this was true or just part of William's larger plot to get Maria to agree to a rushed marriage. Some reports say Maria dressed as a man to sneak away, avoid arrest, and meet William on the night they were to elope. Did William suggest the disguise so nobody could say they saw Maria that night?

The pair met at the Red Barn on May 18, 1827, and Maria was never seen alive again.

William told the Marten family that there had been an issue with the marriage certificate, but Maria had stayed in Ipswich and was awaiting his return while he tied up loose ends at the farm. Many people in the town were suspicious of him. Maria's family kept asking where and how she was. He told them she was afraid to return home because of the arrest warrant, and the scrutiny she would face from the town.

Having run out of excuses for why he wasn't with his soon-to-be wife, William left town a few weeks after Maria's disappearance. He went to London then visited the Isle of Wight, where he wrote a series of letters to Maria's family telling them the two had finally gotten married and had settled on the island. He made a series of dim-witted excuses as to why they hadn't received any letters directly from Maria. He said she had, in fact, been writing and was puzzled why her letters weren't reaching the family. Later, he claimed Maria had hurt her hand and couldn't write to them, but assured them that everything was fine, and they were happily married.

William returned to London and immediately set about starting a new life. He placed an ad looking for a wife in *The Times*. Out of more than a hundred responses, he chose schoolteacher Mary Moore. They married in November 1827 and opened a school for girls in Ealing.

Back at the Marten household, Maria's stepmother began having strange dreams about Maria's whereabouts. These dreams told her that Maria had been murdered and was buried underneath the Red Barn.

Unable to shake the feeling that the dreams might be real, Ann asked her husband to go search the barn. Right where his wife's dream said Maria would be, he found a mound of disturbed earth. He took the spike he used to catch moles and began digging around under the soil. There he found the corpse of his daughter. She had been strangled with a green handkerchief, shot in the face, and seemingly stabbed in the chest and neck, though these wounds could have come from her father's carelessness with his mole-catching spike.

One theory suggests that Maria's stepmother, being closer in age and looks to William than her old husband, was also having an affair with William. Some speculate that Ann knew what had happened to Maria all along, and was waiting for William to return to town to collect her so they could run away together. When news got to her that William had married someone else in London, she decided to get revenge by exposing the murder.

Ann's dreams did only start after William got married, which was about a year after Maria's death. Although there is no logic to the spirit world, it seems odd that these dreams didn't start sooner.

Regardless of who knew what, the authorities were called, and a manhunt for William ensued. It was not hard to track him down. He was found at the schoolhouse with his new wife. Despite having spent months corresponding with Maria's family, telling them she was alive and well, William told police he didn't know anything about Maria. A French passport was found in his home, suggesting he may have been getting ready to flee the country.

William Corder was arrested for Maria's murder, and a massive media frenzy began immediately. Journalists were certain he was guilty. They wrote salacious articles about the murder, calling him a killer before the trial even began. Articles, books, songs, and plays all came out detailing the crime, while William sat in jail awaiting his trial. Pottery and other memorabilia of the Red Barn were made, and the barn itself was totally ransacked by those looking to own a part of history. Some of the wood from the barn was even sold as toothpicks. Similarly, Maria's grave was chipped away at by these obsessed souvenir hunters.

By the time the trial started on August 7, 1828, William had long since been convicted in the court of public opinion. He even mentioned this to Judge Alexander, who was presiding over the case, saying:

By that powerful engine, the press, which regulates the opinion of so many persons in this country, and which is too often, I fear, though unintentionally, the slanderer and destroyer of innocence, I have had the misfortune to be depicted in the most humiliated and revolting characters! I have been described by that press as the most depraved of human monsters.

A change of location was not granted, and the trial went ahead. William was charged with several counts of murder (by stabbing, strangulation, shooting, and even by burying alive). The rudimentary forensics of the 1800s couldn't determine Maria's actual cause of death, and the court didn't want to risk William getting off on a technicality. He was also being charged with other crimes, such as fraud, just to make sure he went down for something.

Tickets were sold to men in town who wished to watch the trial, while others who couldn't get in waited outside to hear the day's news. People poured into the town from across the country. Hotels were fully booked, and some people simply slept outside. One account said the streets were so full of people, it took court officials thirty minutes to wade through the onlookers and get into the building.

William's defense was that Maria had actually taken her own life at the barn, and he had simply buried her. Of course, this doesn't explain why he lied to her family for months after her death, saying she was alive and happily married. Even if it were an accident, he still very much covered up her death.

Whether the evidence against him was just extremely compelling, or the jury was made up of people who had been caught up in the sensational media storm before the trial, is not entirely clear. Either way, they only deliberated for thirty-five minutes before returning a verdict of 'guilty.'

Judge Alexander sentenced William to hang. His body was then to be dissected and anatomized for medical study, instead of being given a final resting place.

The entire time he was awaiting his fate, William was constantly badgered by court officials for a confession. Eventually, he conceded that he did technically kill Maria, but he had accidentally shot her through the eye, panicked, and buried her. He maintained that he did not stab her, which may have been true, but he didn't explain the handkerchief wrapped around her neck. Again, no explanation of the death excuses the fact that he pretended she was alive for so long afterward.

A mere three days after his conviction, William was hanged in front of a crowd of at least seven thousand spectators (some reports say as many as twenty thousand). His body was left to swing for an hour before it was taken down. His torso was given a long, deep slice down the front, and placed on display for thousands of curious onlookers. He was then totally dissected, and his skeleton was made into a medical prop.

The hangman continued to capitalize on the morbid fascination with the crime and sold parts of the rope he had used to hang William. Others followed suit and auctioned things like a lock of Maria's hair and parts of the barn. Somehow William's scalp and one of his ears were taken from the dissection and ended up on display at a museum in London.

Perhaps most gruesomely, William's skin was removed, tanned, and used to bind a book that detailed his crime.

It soon became clear that William's spirit was not happy with the way his body had been treated. Dr. John Kilner, a devoted follower of the crime who owned a lot of memorabilia from the Red Barn, bought—or possibly stole—William's skull. He immediately started having bad luck, hearing voices, and thinking he saw ghosts.

One night, Kilner said he heard a loud noise coming from downstairs as he lay in bed. When he investigated, he found that the cabinet where he kept the skull had opened by itself, the box the skull was kept in was cracked, and the skull itself was on the other side of the room. Kilner was certain that the skull was cursed by the unhappy spirit of the killer. He paid to have a proper Catholic burial for the skull, giving William a final resting place.

The rest of William's body remained on display at the Hunterian Museum in London until 2004, when Corder descendants requested it be taken down and cremated.

Otto in the Attic:
The Bat Man of Milwaukee

On August 22, 1922, Fred Oesterreich was having a particularly heated argument with his wife, Walburga 'Dolly' Oesterreich. Suddenly, he was faced with the impossible appearance of a man who had worked for him almost a decade ago, in a city over 2,000 miles away. Why he was there, and what happened next, revealed one of the most salacious and bizarre love stories the nation had ever seen.

Dolly was born in 1880 in Germany. She and her family moved to the United States, and she grew up poor, on a Midwest farm. In her early twenties, she married a wealthy apron factory owner in Milwaukee, Fred Oesterreich. Fred was both a workaholic and an alcoholic, leaving Dolly alone and sexually unsatisfied most of the time.

One hot summer day in 1913, Dolly told Fred that her

sewing machine was broken and asked him to send someone to repair it. She knew Fred would send Otto Sanhuber, the seventeen-year-old repair boy who worked at the factory. Otto had caught Dolly's eye during a visit to the factory, and she was eager to see him again.

When Otto arrived, Dolly answered the door in nothing but a robe and stockings. From that moment on, Dolly and Otto were embroiled in an affair. At first, they took the usual option deployed when someone is sneaking around behind their spouse's back: they met at hotel rooms and tried their hardest to keep their dealings a secret. Soon, that got to be too much work, and Otto just came over to the Oesterreich house to have sex in Dolly and Fred's bed.

Dolly's neighbors started noticing this strange man who definitely wasn't her husband visiting the home often. She told them he was her 'vagabond half-brother' to slough off any suspicion that she was cheating on Fred. Eventually, Dolly realized that her nosey neighbors knew too much, and Otto couldn't keep coming over so obviously.

Instead of stopping the affair, or going back to meeting secretly at hotels, Dolly suggested that Otto quit his job at the factory and move into the Oesterreichs' attic. For some reason, Otto agreed to this absurd arrangement.

Even more absurd, it went on for five years. Otto lived in the attic, never venturing out unless it was to have sex with Dolly. He spent his free time writing pulp fiction stories and even managed to get some published under a pen name.

Fred, a severe alcoholic, didn't really notice much for a

long time. He did think he was going mad, or even being haunted, as Otto reached his five-year attic anniversary. Fred thought he heard noises coming from upstairs, saw shadows out of the corner of his eye, and noticed that his cigars were disappearing.

This not-entirely misplaced paranoia led Fred to want to move out of the Milwaukee home. He suggested to Dolly that they move to Los Angeles. This was the perfect opportunity for Dolly to come clean about the affair, or let Otto go and live his own life. However, that didn't happen. Dolly found a house in L.A. with an attic and sent Otto ahead to set up his attic space before she and the still-oblivious Fred moved in.

Otto spent another four years living in the Oesterreichs' attic, his only activities being writing and sex with Dolly.

Then came that August day in 1922. Otto heard Dolly and Fred arguing on the floor below. Afraid Fred would hurt her, he jumped down from his hiding space holding two pistols. The men fought, and Otto ended up firing three bullets into Fred's chest, killing him.

Dolly panicked, knowing the neighbors would probably have heard gunshots and called the police. How was she going to explain any of this odd scene? Otto and Dolly agreed to stage the room to look like a botched burglary. Otto locked Dolly in the closet and took the key, along with the murder weapon, back up to his attic.

The police arrived to find Fred dead, and Dolly locked up. She said someone had broken in, shoved her in the closet,

THE MOST BIZARRE TRUE CRIME STORIES EVER TOLD

shot Fred, and stolen a bunch of valuables, including Fred's diamond watch.

With Fred out of the picture, you would expect Otto to just move into the main house and be with Dolly officially. However, Otto continued to live up in the attic. In fact, Dolly even moved out of the house where her husband was killed, and Otto followed her—to live in her new attic!

Dolly began several affairs with different men around town. She started seeing lawyer Herman S. Shapiro, and a man named Roy Klumb. It seems that she was just dating Klumb so that he would help her to dispose of the murder weapon. She told him she owned a gun that was very similar to the one the robber had used to murder Fred, and wanted Klumb to get rid of it, lest she be implicated in the murder. He threw it in the La Brea Tar Pits.

One source says she also convinced a neighbor to bury the other pistol Otto was holding that night in his backyard.

As Dolly's relationship with Shapiro progressed, she gifted him a diamond watch—the same diamond watch she told police her husband's murderer had stolen from the house. Shapiro brought this up with her, and she said she had later found it under a couch cushion but hadn't felt the need to report it to the police.

Meanwhile, Dolly had gotten what she needed from Klumb and had unceremoniously broken up with him. As revenge, Klumb went to the police with the information about the gun he had disposed of at Dolly's request.

Dolly was arrested based on Klumb's story. The tar pits were dredged and the gun was found, though it was badly corroded. While awaiting her hearing, Dolly told Shapiro about her 'half-brother' who lived in her attic and asked him to bring him groceries. She said all he had to do was 'tap on the ceiling of the bedroom closet to let him know he should come out.'

Shapiro did what Dolly asked. But having not spoken to another human besides Dolly for almost a decade, Otto excitedly spilled his guts about the real nature of his relationship with Dolly. Shapiro told him to leave the house and get out of town. Otto left and briefly moved to Canada.

Because the gun evidence was so damaged, and police still couldn't explain how Dolly would have ended up locked in the closet if she had killed Fred, she was released.

Shapiro was apparently not turned off by the murder suspicion or the weird relationship with an attic man. He moved in with Dolly, and they lived happily for the next seven years. As their relationship started deteriorating, though, Shapiro followed in Klumb's footsteps and decided to get revenge by going to the police with what he knew about Otto, and Fred's death.

Once again Dolly was taken into custody, and a warrant went out for Otto's arrest. Weirdly, he had just moved back to L.A. from Canada and was brought in by the police.

Otto was found guilty of manslaughter. However, the statute of limitations for convicting that crime was seven years, and it had already been eight. Otto walked free. He continued writing and, as far as anyone can tell, didn't go live in anyone else's attic.

Dolly's trial ended in a hung jury, and the charges were eventually dropped in 1936. She took another lover, and lived with him in harmony until she died in 1961, at eighty years old.

Arne Cheyenne Johnson, The 'Devil Made Me Do It' Case

We've all had unfortunate moments when we've felt that we didn't act like ourselves; we snap at friends, are rude to strangers, or just generally act out of character. Normally, though, these bouts of strange behavior don't end in someone being stabbed to death. Arne Cheyenne Johnson couldn't say the same.

In July of 1980, Arne Cheyenne Johnson (who went by Cheyenne) and his fiancée, Debbie Glatzel, were clearing out the yard of a rental property in their small Connecticut town of Brookfield. Debbie had brought her eleven-year-old brother, David, along to help. A little while into the job, David came to the couple looking terrified. He said he had been cleaning up near the old well on the property and had seen a suspicious old man. Later, when David was alone in the bedroom of the house, the man appeared again, punched David onto the waterbed, and threatened to harm his family if they moved into the house.

From then on, David began having horrific night terrors and waking up with mysterious bruises and scratches. David said he had dreams of the old man from the rental property, with a white beard, wearing the same jeans and a flannel shirt, only he was 'burnt and black-looking.' The dreams graduated to waking visions. David saw the old man appearing in broad daylight, becoming more and more twisted and demonic until he was described as having 'big black eyes, a thin face with animal features and jagged teeth, pointed ears, horns, and hoofs.'

The rest of the Glatzel family also started hearing weird noises coming from the attic. They were sure something demonic was happening. The Glatzels called a priest to bless the house, but it was not enough to stop David's visions. David was also assessed by a psychologist who allegedly told the family he was 'normal' with a 'minimal learning disability.' But what David was experiencing certainly couldn't be attributed to a simple learning disability.

After twelve days of horror, the family reached out to famous demonologists Ed and Lorraine Warren, who had also been involved in the Amityville Horror case. When they visited, Ed immediately started experiencing paranormal events. He heard growling and banging from the basement and saw objects move on their own. Various sources have claimed that the family rocking chair would randomly start rocking with nobody in it, one of David's toy dinosaurs walked across the floor by itself, and a cake levitated, leaving frosting on the ceiling. At one point the whole family heard a deep, disembodied voice say, 'Beware, you're all going to die.'

Meanwhile, Lorraine, the psychic medium of the Warren duo, saw a physical manifestation of what she assumed to be the entity terrorizing David. She said, 'While Ed interviewed the boy I saw a black, misty form next to him, which told me we were dealing with something of a negative nature.' Usually ghosts of human spirits are said to appear as humans and are not considered dangerous to the living. Dark mists, and twisted figures like those that David had been seeing, are thought to be signs of the demonic.

The entity didn't seem to enjoy the presence of the Warrens and seemingly started to ramp up its efforts to harm David. He began to feel like invisible hands were choking him, and red finger-like marks started appearing on his neck. He also said he had 'the feeling of being hit,' even when nobody was standing near enough to touch him.

As the days went on, David got much worse. Lorraine reported that David spoke in unrecognizable voices, reciting passages from the Bible and John Milton's *Paradise Lost*. He growled, hissed, and swore—and tried to bite and kick anyone who came near him. Debbie claimed that when the entity had a hold of him, it would 'flop him rapidly head-to-toe like a rag doll.'

Multiple priests came to bless the home and assess David. None of them thought they could help enough, so a formal exorcism was requested from the Church. For what it's worth, the Diocese of Bridgeport does confirm that several of their priests helped David out. A spokesperson for the organization said, 'No one from the church has said one way or the other what was involved, and we decline to say.' In other words, they won't outright deny that an exorcism took place.

According to Lorraine's account, David continued to snarl, hiss, and talk in strange voices during his exorcism. At one point, he allegedly levitated and stopped breathing.

Cheyenne was there for the whole terrifying process. At one point, he made what Ed would call a fatal mistake, by taunting the demon. He yelled at it, 'Take me on, leave my little buddy alone!' Several witnesses claimed to have seen the demon leap from David's body into Cheyenne's.

Once the exorcism was complete, David began to feel better. He no longer had visions of the old man, he regained his energy and his normal personality, and the red marks disappeared.

However, this was not the end of the trouble for the family. As David got better, Cheyenne started getting worse. He had a string of bad luck, and two significant accidents: he fell out of a tree while doing a landscaping job and he inexplicably lost control of his car and hit a tree. These could be considered mere coincidences or they could have been caused by a simple lack of focus thanks to high stress levels and little sleep. After all, he had just witnessed a turbulent exorcism and was grappling with the possibility of the existence of demons. That would distract anyone. However, Cheyenne maintains that these accidents were the work of the demon.

Cheyenne and Debbie decided not to move into the rental property where David had first encountered the old man. However, despite being warned against ever returning to that place, Cheyenne admitted he went back and looked in the well that the demon had supposedly made its earthly home. There he said he looked the demon in the eyes and became fully possessed. He claims looking in the well was the last time he was fully lucid until after the murder he was about to commit.

The couple moved into an apartment owned by Alan Bono, Debbie's manager at the dog grooming kennel where she worked. The trio were allegedly good friends and would often spend time together.

On February 16, 1981, Cheyenne, Debbie, and Alan, along with Cheyenne's sister, Wanda, and Debbie's nine-year-old cousin, Mary, went to lunch at a pub in town. The adults of the party had a few drinks and spent a lovely afternoon together, though Wanda noted later that Alan got significantly drunker than the others.

Afterward, they returned to Alan's apartment over the dog kennel. Alan had hired Cheyenne to fix his stereo, so he got to work on that, while Alan kept drinking. Debbie said the two men, probably encouraged by the alcohol, had a heated dispute over the payment for this job.

Debbie took the girls out for pizza while the men hashed out their issues, but rushed back because she thought something bad might happen if they were left alone too long. When they returned, Alan still seemed to be in a heightened, angry state. He kept punching his left palm with his right fist, and he looked drunk and annoyed.

Debbie wanted to get the young girls away from Alan, who was obviously disturbed, so they began to gather their things and leave. Alan, not wanting the party to end, grabbed nine-year-old Mary. Cheyenne came back into the apartment from outside and told Alan to let Mary go. The young girl ran for the car, while Debbie and Wanda stayed behind to try and prevent a fight between the two men.

Cheyenne seemed to fall into a kind of trance as he began to attack Alan. Wanda said she attempted to pull him away but said, 'he was like a stone ... I couldn't budge him.' Suddenly Cheyenne, still growling like a vicious animal, pulled his five-inch pocket knife out and stabbed Alan. Cheyenne's lawyer later described Alan's injuries as 'four or five tremendous wounds.'

Wanda recalls the attack stopping very suddenly, and Cheyenne calmly walking away, into the woods, with a blank expression on his face. A few hours later, Alan died of his injuries, and Cheyenne was found two miles away from the crime scene.

When Lorraine heard about the murder, she immediately called the police station and told them it was certainly a case of demonic possession. She and Ed returned to Bridgeport to help the police.

The trial began on October 28, 1981, at Connecticut's

Superior Court. The press had caught wind of the accusations of demonic possession and were eager to see what the court would do with such an outlandish claim.

Cheyenne's lawyer, Martin Minella, did indeed attempt to enter a plea of 'not guilty by reason of demonic possession,' saying his client 'was possessed by a demon, and it was a demon who actually manipulated his body.' It was the first time in U.S. history that anyone had tried to claim possession in a courtroom.

Minella astutely said, 'The courts have dealt with the existence of God. Now they're going to have to deal with the existence of the Devil.' Was it really that wild of a claim? Didn't many witnesses swear on a Bible to tell the truth? If the court was willing to allow such blatant acknowledgment of the Christian God, then why would mentioning the Devil be off-limits?

Judge Robert Callahan immediately threw out the plea, claiming that any testimony relating to demonic possession would be 'unscientific' and therefore 'irrelative' to the verdict. Yes, the existence of God is allowed to be alluded to in a court but not as it actually pertains to a case. Simply swearing on a Bible, if you are religious and choose to do so, is very different from attempting to prove the existence of God beyond reasonable doubt. Similarly, the court could allude to the Devil, but actually trying to prove not only that he exists, but also that he possessed someone to commit a murder, would be a completely different thing.

The court was not looking for an affirmation of faith, they

were dealing with a murder, which had very blatantly been committed by (at least the body of) Arne Cheyenne Johnson.

The trial went forward with the jury instructed to banish the possibility of demonic possession from their minds. Though some witnesses to David's exorcism did testify that they saw the demon come out of David and enter Cheyenne, and many friends and family members told the court that Cheyenne hadn't been the same since that day, the jury couldn't get around the fact that Cheyenne was the one who killed Alan.

After a three-day deliberation, the jury came back with a verdict of 'guilty.' On November 24, 1981, Cheyenne was convicted of first-degree manslaughter, and sentenced to ten to twenty years in prison.

In prison, he earned his high school diploma and got married to Debbie, who still maintained that Cheyenne had been possessed during the murder, and stood by him. Cheyenne only ended up serving five years of his sentence and was released in 1986. The couple went on to have two kids and have never reported any further demonic activity.

While many involved in the incidents still believe the Devil was involved, David Glatzel and his brother Carl think the only demons were the Warrens. Lorraine Warren co-authored a book with Gerald Brittle about the incident called *The Devil in Connecticut*. Carl called it a 'complete lie' and said, 'the Warrens concocted a phony story about demons in an attempt to get rich and famous at our expense.'

In 2007, David and Carl sued the authors of the book, as

well as the publishers, for libel and 'intentional infliction of emotional distress.' Both authors stick by their story. Brittle claims his book is based in fact, and that all the information came from over a hundred hours of interviews he did with the Glatzel family, and those involved in the exorcism. Lorraine said every one of the priests involved also maintains that David was possessed by a demon.

The Circleville Letter Writer

In March 1977, school bus driver Mary Gillespie began getting strange letters mailed to her home in the small town of Circleville, Ohio. They were written in all capital letters, slanted slightly to the right. They were all postmarked from Columbus, about thirty miles north of Circleville, but had no return address.

These letters accused Mary of having an affair with the superintendent of schools for the district, Gordon Massie, and threatened that she needed to come clean. The first letter read: 'Stay away from Massie. Don't lie when questioned about knowing him. I know where you live. I've been observing your house and know you have children. This is no joke. Please take it serious [sic]. Everyone concerned has been notified, and everything will be over soon.'

Mary claims she had no clue what the letter was referring to, but was disturbed that the writer seemed to know intimate details about her home and her kids. Mary knew of Gordon, as they both worked for the school board, and lived in a town with a population of only about 14,000 people, but she insists she wasn't having an affair with him.

Mary didn't know what to do, so she just ignored the letter. She didn't even initially tell her husband Ron about it. She just wanted to put it behind her. However, the letters kept coming.

The second letter was much more aggressive and alarmingly specific. It included the number of Mary's bus and the exact details of her bus route. It also threatened to 'put a bullet in that little girl's head,' referring to Mary and Ron's young daughter, Traci.

A third letter arrived, saying it was Mary's 'last chance to report' Gordon for having an affair with her. This letter did have a return address, 550 Ridgewood Drive, right there in Circleville. That home belonged to Gordon Massie and his wife.

Of course, Gordon wasn't the one writing these letters accusing himself of having an affair. It turned out that he had also been receiving creepy letters accusing him of an affair with Mary. The writer continued to threaten that they would tell the school board of Gordon and Mary's wrongdoings if they didn't admit it themselves. The writer didn't seem to be keeping up with their own lore, though, as some letters claimed that they had already written to the appropriate people to inform them of the affair.

Soon letters started being delivered all over town. Some

people on the school board did indeed receive letters 'exposing' Gordon and Mary. Churches, stores, newspapers, and random townspeople also received the strange notes. Mary's husband Ron even got one that suggested he kill his wife and her secret lover.

Nobody was sure what to do. Hundreds of letters were being received all over town demanding a confession to something that wasn't true and giving no other instructions for how to make the campaign end.

One letter warned Mary that the writer was going to increase the heat. They claimed they were going to start putting up signs all around town telling her alleged story. As promised, cardboard signs with the same writing, and same accusations, started popping up all around Circleville, with most being posted on Mary's school bus route.

The signs and letters turned viler as they also accused Gordon of an inappropriate sexual relationship with Mary's daughter. The Gillespies were desperate for Traci not to see anything that involved such lewd accusations, so Ron got up early every morning to drive around and take the signs down before anyone could see them.

Ron's sister Karen and her husband, Paul Freshour, visited the Gillespie home to try and come up with a plan to stop the madness.

Mary recalled an incident where another bus driver, David Longberry, had made a pass at her, and she'd rejected him. She thought maybe this was his deranged way of getting revenge on her. They decided they should write their own note to David, telling him they knew he was the writer, and he wasn't going to coerce a confession out of anyone, so he might as well stop this ridiculous plan.

Their plan seemed to work. Mary stopped getting letters, and no signs on the road appeared for several weeks.

On August 19, 1977, the case took a mysterious and tragic turn. Mary and her sister-in-law Karen were out of town on a girls' trip. Mary's daughter Traci recalls that around 10 p.m. the phone rang, and her father spoke briefly but intensely with the person on the other end. He hung up and told Traci he was going to confront the letter writer. Ron got his gun out and drove away.

Less than ten miles from the Gillespie house, Ron had a serious accident. It appeared he had almost missed a turn, swerved to try and make it, lost control of the car, and crashed. Ron suffered massive internal injuries and died before he got to the hospital. He apparently had a blood alcohol concentration of .16, almost double the legal limit. Ron's gun was found in the car and was missing a bullet, though there was no indication that he had fired it that night, just that it had been used at some point.

This was all suspicious to a lot of people who knew Ron. Ron was familiar with the area, and it seemed odd that he would miss the turn he took almost every day. The weather was good that night, too: clear and dry. It was unlikely that the roads were slippery or that his visibility was diminished. Ron also wasn't much of a drinker. At five foot seven inches and 155 pounds, it would take four or five drinks to reach that blood alcohol concentration. His family said Ron was not the type to sit around having five drinks on a casual night at home, especially when he was the only parent in the state at the time. Traci also said he didn't seem drunk as he left the house.

Ron's brother-in-law, Paul Freshour, spoke to Sheriff Dwight Radcliff at the scene of the crash. He later said that the sheriff told him he was reluctant to definitively call it an accident. When Paul spoke to him a few days later, though, he said a suspect had been cleared, and he was now more comfortable with labeling the crash an accident. The sheriff didn't tell Paul who had been suspected or why, or how they had been cleared.

Once Ron's crash was officially designated an accident, and his cause of death was released to the public, the letters began again. This time they were targeting Sheriff Radcliff, saying he was covering up what really happened to Ron. The writer told the town that Mary and Gordon were responsible for Ron's death. Whether or not the writer knew that Mary hadn't even been in the state at the time is unclear, but it didn't seem to matter.

A two-year period of silence followed these accusations. Mary was able to grieve the untimely death of her husband, and was cautiously optimistic that it would be the end of the mysterious letter writer.

However, in the fall of 1979, the letters started up once again. By this time, Gordon Massie and his wife were getting a divorce. Oddly enough, Mary and Gordon had started actually having an affair. Both swear it happened after the letters accusing them of it and after Ron's death. They said bonding over the letters is what brought them close in the first place, so the accusations had manifested the real thing, rather than the other way around.

In 1982 Karen and Paul also separated. Karen said Paul was physically abusive in their relationship and had given her black eyes and wounds needing stitches. She described him as 'manipulative,' and mentioned to Mary that he might be the one writing the letters. Karen had discovered similar letters to the ones everyone had been receiving in her house, and even found one clogging the toilet.

Paul had apparently really turned on Mary at some point in her relationship with Ron. Paul allegedly believed the accusations of the affair, and blamed Mary for Ron's death. The Freshour divorce became bitter over custody of their children and some valuable assets, so many believe Karen's accusations were simply made out of spite and weren't necessarily grounded in any real evidence.

The letters continued.

Traci Gillespie now became the target of the menacing letter writer. She received vile, sexually explicit letters. The signs that had once again started being posted on the roads again accused Gordon and the thirteen-year-old Traci of having a sexual relationship.

On Monday, February 7, 1983, the case took another grim turn. In between dropping off and picking up kids along her bus route, Mary saw another sign saying horrific things about her daughter. She parked the bus, got out, and went to rip the sign down. Behind it she found a strange contraption: a box with some wood and a series of strings attached to it. She took the whole thing with her, hoping to find some clues as to who was terrorizing her family.

Mary finished her bus route as normal, then sat in her driveway and investigated the box. The lid was glued shut, but as she pried it open, she was shocked at what she found: a .25 caliber handgun, held up with Styrofoam, with strings attached to the trigger. At first, she thought maybe it was not real, or at least not loaded, but further investigation proved that it was both. She took the box and the gun to the police, and they confirmed that the intention was for the gun to have fired when someone took the sign in front of it down. The letter writer had just tried to murder Mary Gillespie.

The serial number of the gun had been partially filed off, but the police crime lab was able to lift it anyway. They tracked down the sale to a Columbus gun shop. Management said it had been purchased by a man named Wesley Wells. When police spoke to Wesley, he said he had sold the gun to his supervisor a year earlier. His supervisor was Paul Freshour.

The police investigation discovered that Paul had taken the morning off work on the day that Mary found the booby-trapped box.

On February 25, 1983, Paul was taken into custody and questioned. Sheriff Radcliff asked him about the gun, and he said he had bought it from Wesley, but claimed he hadn't seen it since he got back from a vacation in January. He said he didn't report it missing because he thought a family member had taken it and he didn't want to get them in trouble. He refused to tell police who that family member was.

Paul took three or four polygraph tests and failed each one. He was also asked to give several writing samples, and some were taken from his work files. Radcliff is often criticized for getting Paul to copy the letters word-for-word in the same style. Usually, when handwriting samples are taken, the person is dictated what to write, not actually given the evidence to copy. Some feel like Paul was being set up. His samples were found to be a match to many of the letters and postcards that were sent from the letter writer. However, the samples used in court were ones that had been dictated, and some from his personal correspondence. None of the directly copied letters made it into evidence.

Radcliff was also criticized for not following up on a promising lead. Another bus driver on Mary's route saw someone near the site of the trap not long before Mary must have found it. He had 'sandy blond hair,' and was driving a yellow or orange El Camino. Some sources claim that this vehicle can be connected to the person Mary originally thought was sending the letters, David Longberry. His brother allegedly had the same car.

In 1999, Longberry was caught raping an eleven-year-old-girl and fled town. He committed suicide before he could be tracked down. The letter writer had been saying sexually explicit things about Mary's underage daughter for years, and Longberry did have a reason to target Mary, but this lead was never investigated.

A grand jury indicted Paul for attempted murder in March 1983. While awaiting the trial, set to start in October, Paul was let out on bail and checked himself into a psychiatric facility. It isn't clear whether this was a legitimate stay, due to the stress of the situation and his crumbling marriage, or if he was just trying to set himself up for an insanity plea. Paul's defense did briefly submit a plea of not guilty by virtue of insanity, but it was later rescinded.

The trial lasted twelve days. Thirty-nine of the more than one thousand letters the town had received were admitted into evidence. The jury saw that Paul's handwriting was a match to the letters, that the gun belonged to him, and that he had taken the morning of February 7 off work. Paul's defense said it was Karen, looking for revenge over their hostile custody proceedings, who had set up the trap. Paul also had alibis that checked out for part of the morning he took off work.

However, the evidence against Paul was too compelling for the jury. They didn't see why Karen would risk harming Mary just to get revenge on Paul. It was also wildly suspicious that it was his gun that was used, and that he had such a weak and confusing excuse for why it wasn't in his possession at the time.

After just a three-hour deliberation, the jury found Paul Freshour guilty of attempted murder. He was sentenced to seven to twenty-five years in jail.

The town of Circleville, Ohio breathed a collective sigh of relief as the suspected writer who had terrorized them all for years was sent to prison. Surely that would be the end of the ordeal?

Unfortunately, this was not to be the case. The letters kept coming. Even Paul received one in jail, saying, 'Now when are you going to believe you aren't going to get out of there? I told you 2 years ago. When we set 'em up, they stay set up. Don't you listen at all?'

Paul insisted he had nothing to do with it. The letters still looked the same and were still postmarked from Columbus, while Paul was being held in prison in Lima. Many insisted he must have been smuggling the letters out somehow or that he had an accomplice on the outside who'd sent Paul a letter to throw the authorities off his trail.

Sheriff Radcliff called the warden of the prison and insisted Paul be put in solitary confinement with absolutely no access to other prisoners or a phone, and certainly not a pen and paper. The warden complied with this request but still the letters did not stop. There was no possible way that Paul was still the one sending letters, yet he remained in prison for the crime. He hadn't been arrested for writing letters, after all. He had been convicted of attempted murder.

Paul was granted parole in 1994, after ten years in prison. He still vehemently denied being the letter writer and even put together a massive 162-page report on all the letters the town received to send to the FBI to request a proper investigation.

In the mid nineties, *Unsolved Mysteries* aired an episode about the letter writer. They soon received their own letter, warning them away from investigating any further. It read, 'Forget Circleville, Ohio ... if you come to Ohio, you el sickos will pay. The Circleville Writer.'

After that, nobody ever received a letter from the Circleville letter writer again. Paul Freshour died in 2012, still adamant that he was not the culprit.

Katarzyna Zowada and the Buffalo Bill Murderer

In the horror film *The Silence of the Lambs*, a murderer nicknamed 'Buffalo Bill' kidnaps women, starves them in a pit until their skin is loose, then removes their flesh and wears it as a costume. Though the character was partly inspired by real-life criminal Ed Gein, who fashioned lampshades and face masks out of skin, Gein got most of his materials from robbing graves, not capturing and torturing people. The Buffalo Bill skin suit remained a thing of legend; that is, until 1998.

Katarzyna Zowada was a student at the Jagiellonian University in Kraków. She'd had a hard few years, struggling with depression since her father died. Katarzyna felt she was responsible for his death. She had insisted the two go on a hike together, where he had fallen and suffered a spinal injury that later killed him. Katarzyna felt a great amount of guilt about this and freely agreed to go to counseling.

Katarzyna seemed to have a difficult time finding her path in life. She initially studied psychology, then switched to history, and finally settled on religious studies. Her classmates say her attendance was a little spotty and that she was a shy, reserved person who they didn't really know much about.

While her school attendance may have been inconsistent, her therapy attendance was not. She dutifully showed up to every session, eager to find some relief from her guilt and sadness. On November 12, 1998, her mother waited for her outside the psychiatry clinic in the Nowa Huta neighborhood of Kraków where Katarzyna had a 6 p.m. therapy appointment. She never arrived.

Katarzyna's mother started calling around to family and friends, but nobody had seen Katarzyna. She went to the police, but was told that because of her depressed state of mind, it was likely that Katarzyna was out partying with friends, or that she had run away, as many depressed young women do. Despite her instance that her daughter wouldn't do that, Katarzyna's mother was told she couldn't file a missing person's report until Katarzyna had been missing for twenty-four hours.

When the investigation did begin, it didn't turn up many leads. Police noted that Katarzyna had been attempting to change her appearance over the few months before her disappearance. She had dyed her hair blonde and had lost some weight. Classmates said her attendance had been dropping even further, leading police to believe that Katarzyna had met someone recently and had been having a secret relationship with them, though they had no leads as to who this person might be. CCTV footage from her usual hang-out spots didn't catch any glimpses of her.

On January 6, 1999, a tugboat called the *Elk* got something stuck in its propellor while sailing on the Vistula River. The boat workers thought it was some sort of giant rubber band or leathery material. It was actually a much more horrifying item. As the workers looked closer, they saw that it was human remains that had been fashioned into a skin suit. DNA tests confirmed it was the body of Katarzyna.

The river was dredged and some of Kataryna's clothes and her right leg were found, though the rest of her body was still missing.

Because of the precision of the butchery, and the fact that her flesh had been fashioned into a suit intended for someone to wear, police deduced that the killer was likely a butcher, surgeon, or hunter, and was probably close to the same size as Katarzyna. They were probably an intelligent killer who chose his victims ahead of time and likely stalked them, rather than a frenzied opportunistic person who killed whoever they could find. Other than that, the police had no solid leads.

In May 1999, police received a call from a distressed elderly man saying he thought his grandson had killed someone. The elderly man, who had very poor eyesight, said he felt something was strange about his grandson's appearance. When police arrived at the home, where the caller was living with his son and grandson, they found a gruesome scene. The corpse of the caller's fifty-year-old son was hanging upside down from the rafters. His head had been skinned, and the caller's grandson was wearing his father's face as a mask and was dressed in his clothes.

Police identified the killer as Vladimir W. He was arrested for the murder of his father and seemed like a good lead in the case of Katarzyna. After all, how many killers interested in skinning their victims and using their flesh to dress up as them could there possibly be in Poland at one time?

It turned out that Vladimir and Katarzyna both went to the same university and had both studied psychology at one point, but there was no concrete evidence that they had ever met, and nothing else linking Vladimir to Katarzyna's murder. Vladimir insisted he knew nothing of Katarzyna, and was deported to his native Russia to serve a twenty-five-year sentence for his crimes against his father.

Vladimir was the first and only solid lead the detectives were to get for two decades.

In 2012, thanks to more sophisticated DNA testing and modeling, investigators were able to create a 3D model of Katarzyna's body before she was skinned. They also determined some extremely disturbing details about the last moments of her life.

Katarzyna had been chained up by her ankles, beaten, and tortured for weeks before she died. She most likely had a shattered pelvis from multiple beatings with a heavy object. Worst of all, she was probably skinned alive, before being dismembered and having her flesh fashioned into the skin suit that was found in the river. There was also evidence that she was raped after her death.

Because of some of the marks found on her body, the authorities added that the perpetrator may have been trained in martial arts to their criminal profile.

In 2017, the police received a letter which led to their next big lead. It had come from a friend of a man named Robert Janczewski, who had been becoming increasingly suspicious of Janczewski's interest in Katarzyna's case. The letter said he had visited her grave several times and didn't live far from the river where her remains were found.

Janczewski had already been on the police's radar; They had been staking out Katarzyna's grave to look for any suspicious people who may want to re-visit their victim and had noticed that Janczewski came a lot.

He also perfectly fit the description of the killer made by criminal profilers. Apparently, when Janczewski was younger, he had enjoyed torturing and killing small animals. He was very antisocial as a child and was called a 'freak' and a 'weirdo' by his classmates. He was trained in martial arts. He had worked in the morgue of the military hospital when he was in the army and later worked in a lab at the Institute of Zoology and Biomedical Research at the Jagiellonian University, where animal testing was being done. He was fired from that position for killing all the rabbits in the lab. Janczewski was also a Peeping Tom and a known harasser of women.

Investigators tore Janczewski's apartment apart and found

blood and hair in his drains and under appliances in his bathroom that matched Katarzyna's.

Robert Janczewski was arrested and charged with aggravated murder with particular cruelty, though not much is known about what happened next. The authorities requested a closed trial and have not released much information. In 2018, Robert made a complaint that he was being harassed by the guards in prison. It was briefly looked into, though nothing came of that investigation.

He remains in prison. The rest of Katarzyna's body was never found.

The Greenbrier Ghost

There is a popular urban legend that tells a tale of a woman who always wore a ribbon around her neck. People would tease her about her constant accessory, but she still never took it off. She warned people they wouldn't like what they saw if she removed it. One day, a prankster decided to snatch it from her. All the eager onlookers' faces fell as they saw the woman's neck bend, and her head fall off her body. Of course, that's just a playground story told to scare children, but it's not entirely unlike the real-life story of Elva Zona Heaster Shue.

On January 23, 1897, blacksmith Erasmus 'Edward' Shue sent eleven-year-old Andy Jones, a young neighbor boy who often ran errands for him, to his home to see if his new wife, Zona, needed anything from the market.

The boy walked into the home in Greenbrier County, West Virginia, expecting Zona to be happily going about her wifely duties and awaiting her husband's return. Instead, he found her body lying lifeless on the floor at the foot of the stairs. She was lying straight out with her legs together, with one arm across her chest, and one by her side. From the way she was lying, it certainly didn't look like she had simply slipped and fallen down the stairs.

Andy was confused and thought she might have just decided to take a nap on the floor. He walked toward her, gently calling her name. When he got no reply, and the realization that she might be dead crept up on him, Andy got scared and ran from the Shue household. He skipped telling Edward Shue about his wife and went straight to his mother, who then called Dr. George W. Knapp to the scene.

It took about an hour for Dr. Knapp to get to the Shue house. In the meantime, Edward had gotten wind of the terrible scene Andy had found in his home. Wanting his new wife to have some dignity before Dr. Knapp came over and examined her, Edward took Zona's body upstairs, washed her, and dressed her in a high-neck dress with a stiff collar. He also placed a veil over her face.

Dr. Knapp arrived to find a very distressed Edward wanting a swift examination and a quick determination of her cause of death. He hovered over her body as the doctor looked over her, getting very agitated if he got near Zona's neck or head. The doctor said he didn't want to upset the grieving widower and assumed that he was just being protective of her body. Dr. Knapp determined that Elva had died of 'everlasting faint,' which, in modern terms, is somewhat akin to a heart attack.

Zona's body was taken to her childhood home in Little

Sewell Mountain, West Virginia, so that her family could attend her funeral and bury her nearby.

At her funeral, Edward was again acting very odd and was pacing back and forth at the head of the open casket. He fussed with her veil and collar, and added a heavy scarf around her neck, insisting it was her favorite and she would have wanted to be buried in it.

Again, everyone in attendance gave him the benefit of the doubt for his weird behavior and assumed he was just grieving and being protective of his wife's body. That is, everyone except Elva's mother, Mary Jane Heaster. Mary had never liked Edward and was convinced he had something to do with her death.

Mary prayed to God for weeks that Zona would return to her somehow and reveal the truth of her death. Weeks later, Mary had four dreams in row in which Zona appeared to her. In the first one, she appeared as a bright light, and she gradually took shape over the next three nights. Zona told her mother that Edward had abused her and had viciously attacked her one night when he thought she hadn't cooked any meat for dinner. Zona told her mother that her new husband had broken her neck. Then, as if in a horror movie, Mary said Elva turned her whole head around, so it was sitting backward on her shoulders, and continued to look her mother in the eyes as she walked forward out of the room.

Mary, along with her brother-in-law, Johnson Heaster, went to Prosecutor John A. Preston. She told Preston about her suspicions of Edward, his strange behavior at the funeral, and the series of dreams she had been having. In a frenzy, she told him she knew Zona had appeared to her to 'tell on' Edward.

It is unclear whether Preston believed Mary's story about the dream, or if she was just persistent enough to spur him into action, but he agreed to reopen the case. He began asking questions of people around town. The Shues' neighbors repeated what Mary had said about Edward acting strangely at the funeral. When questioned, Dr. Knapp admitted he hadn't done the most thorough of examinations, as Edward had seemed incredibly distressed.

The testimony from the townspeople, Dr. Knapp's confession, and Mary's insistence all led Preston to order an exhumation of Zona's body for a full autopsy. Shue forcefully objected to the exhumation. He was told that the autopsy would be part of a broader inquest, which he would be forced to attend. Shue was overheard saying that he knew he would be implicated in Zona's death but that 'they will not be able to prove [he] did it.'

The autopsy almost immediately found that Zona had, in fact, been murdered by strangulation.

A local paper, the *Pocahontas Times*, reported: 'On the throat were the marks of fingers indicating that she had been choken [sic]; that the neck was dislocated between the 1st and 2nd vertebrae. The ligaments were torn and ruptured. The windpipe had been crushed to a point in front of the neck.'

The autopsy had played out exactly how Mary's dreams said it would.

Preston began looking into Shue's past for more evidence that he may have committed this crime. The autopsy wasn't enough, as nobody could prove that Shue was the one who had broken his wife's neck.

It turned out Zona was Shue's third wife. His first two wives had also died in mysterious circumstances. His first wife had died after falling from a haystack and also suffered a broken neck. The second had a rock dropped on her from a roof while she was helping her husband repair a chimney.

One report says that Shue had briefly been in jail for stealing a horse, and had told one of his fellow inmates that he planned on having seven wives.

Everything Preston had heard and seen was enough for him to bring Shue to trial. Preston wanted to avoid Mary's testimony about her dreams as he felt it might discredit the case, though Shue's lawyer extensively questioned her about it. Mary steadfastly stuck to her story. No detail ever changed over the intensive interrogation.

The defendant also took the stand, which is unusual in murder trials. He gave a rambling, incoherent, and off-putting testimony in which he asked the jury to 'look into his face and then say if he was guilty.'

The *Greenbrier Independent* stated that Shue's 'testimony, manner, and so forth made an unfavorable impression on the spectators.'

On June 22, 1897, after only an hour and ten minutes of deliberation, the grand jury found Erasmus 'Edward' Shue guilty of murder. They made sure to clarify that it was because of the circumstantial evidence, and not because of a 'ghost's testimony.'

Despite the jury's insistence their conviction had nothing to do with the paranormal, the town still knew that Elva's body would have never been exhumed and re-examined if it weren't for Mary's dreams, and her insistence that something nefarious had happened to her daughter.

In Greenbrier County today, there is a plaque that reads:

Interred in a nearby cemetery is Zona Heaster Shue. Her death in 1897 was presumed natural until her spirit appeared to her mother to describe how she was killed by her husband Edward. Autopsy on the exhumed body verified the apparition's account. Edward, found guilty of murder, was sentenced to state prison.

Indeed, Edward had been sent to prison for his third wife's death and died on March 13, 1900, after an epidemic tore through the prison population.

Charles C. Morgan and the Ecclesiastes Mystery

O n March 22, 1977, mild-mannered family man and escrow agent Charles C. Morgan went missing from the Tucson, Arizona home that he shared with his wife Ruth and his young daughters.

Three days later, at 2 a.m., Charles returned home. He had a plastic cuff around his ankle and a plastic zip-tie around his wrists. He motioned to his throat to indicate that he couldn't speak. Ruth brought him a pen and paper and he wrote that he had a hallucinogenic drug coating his throat that would 'drive him irrevocably insane, or destroy his nervous system and kill him' if he spoke.

Ruth panicked and wanted to call the police, but Charles insisted their whole family would be in danger if anyone alerted the authorities. There is not much information about what the substance might have been, or how Charles recovered from it without triggering the allegedly powerful substance. Over the next week, though, Ruth managed to nurse Charles back to a point where he was able to talk again.

Charles told Ruth he had been working as a secret agent for the U.S. Treasury Department. At the time, the Treasury Department also dealt with matters of domestic safety, only splitting off to form the Department of Homeland Security in 2003. Charles told his wife that the abductors had taken his Treasury I.D., but didn't say anything else about his kidnapping.

Life very briefly returned to (somewhat) normal. Charles seemed very paranoid. He took to wearing a bullet-proof vest, grew a beard to disguise his face, and insisted he take his daughters to and from school.

Two months after he had arrived home the first time, Charles disappeared again.

Nine days later, Ruth received a mysterious call from an unknown woman saying 'Chuck is alright. Ecclesiastes 12: 1–8.' Ruth had no idea what to make of this bizarre phone call or what a Bible passage had to do with her husband's disappearance.

Ecclesiastes 12: 1–8 reads:

> Remember your Creator
>   in the days of your youth,
> before the days of trouble come
>   and the years approach when you will say,
>   'I find no pleasure in them'—

before the sun and the light
    and the moon and the stars grow dark,
    and the clouds return after the rain;
when the keepers of the house tremble,
    and the strong men stoop,
when the grinders cease because they are few,
    and those looking through the windows grow dim;
when the doors to the street are closed
    and the sound of grinding fades;
when people rise up at the sound of birds,
    but all their songs grow faint;
when people are afraid of heights
    and of dangers in the streets;
when the almond tree blossoms
    and the grasshopper drags itself along
    and desire no longer is stirred.
Then people go to their eternal home
    and mourners go about the streets.

Remember him—before the silver cord is severed,
    and the golden bowl is broken;
before the pitcher is shattered at the spring,
    and the wheel broken at the well,
and the dust returns to the ground it came from,
    and the spirit returns to God who gave it.

'Meaningless! Meaningless!' says the Teacher.
    'Everything is meaningless!'

The passage seems to be a plea to remember God and commit to Him in the end times, and to remember that everything we experience on earth is superficial and vain compared to the pleasures of the kingdom of heaven; it gave no real clue as to where Charles was.

On June 18, 1977, Charles was found dead in the middle of the road, forty miles west of his Tucson home, not far from his Mercury Cougar. He was still wearing his bullet-proof vest and had been shot in the back of the head with his own gun.

Investigators found several puzzling clues at the scene. There was a pair of sunglasses near Charles's body that didn't belong to him. In his car, they found multiple weapons and ammunition, as well as one of Charles's teeth, wrapped in a white handkerchief in the back seat. There were also directions to the spot Charles was found, written in his own writing.

Pinned to Charles's underwear, they found a $2 note with a number of strange markings on it. It had a list of seven Hispanic last names starting with the letters A through G: Acevedo, Bejarano, Cajero, Duarte, Encinas, Fuente, and Gradillas. There was also a map of Robles Junction, an area in Arizona between Tucson and the Mexican border that was known for smuggling. The same Bible verse Ruth had been told over the phone, Ecclesiastes 12, was written above the list of names, and arrows pointed to the one and the eight in the serial number.

As odd as all that is, the strangest part was that the cause of death was ruled to be suicide. Charles had gunshot residue on his left hand, but he was right-handed, and there were no fingerprints on the gun, not even Charles's. How could someone shoot themselves in the back of the head with their non-dominant hand, then wipe the prints from the gun after they were dead? And even if that were possible, why would someone choose to end their life in such an awkward and confusing manner?

The end of that Ecclesiastes passage, 'Everything is Meaningless,' may have pointed to Charles being suicidal, but it doesn't make sense of why the woman had called Ruth and said it to her without explaining what she meant. It also doesn't explain anything else at the scene. If Charles had killed himself, what was the purpose of all the rest of the strange evidence left behind?

The main theory about what happened to Charles is that he was, in fact, doing secret government work, and the wrong people caught up with him. His daughter Megan Hidden said, 'My father had a lot of information about people here in Tucson that could have been very detrimental. There was a lot of information about politicians, people who are still alive that work in our government. He had that information and they wanted to silence him.' Having damning information about the higher-ups in Tucson could explain why his mysterious death was simply ruled a suicide and not investigated as a murder.

Before his death, Charles had testified in a secret state investigation investigating illegal activities by a Tucson bank. He was also known to have done some escrow work for organized crime families. Arizona allowed people to purchase property with a blind trust at the time, meaning a representative would do dealings on behalf of a person or organization that the person or organization had no knowledge of. This allowed criminals to buy up real estate as money-laundering operations without the sale of that property being tied back to them.

Two days after Charles was found, the Sheriff's Department got a call from the same woman who had called Ruth. She called herself 'Green Eyes' and told the authorities that she had met Charles in a motel room, and he had shown her a briefcase full of cash that he said he was going to use to buy the contract that had been put out on his life. The investigation had determined that Charles had spent a week at a Northside motel before he died, but they could not confirm whether or not he had a large briefcase of cash, or whether the woman had met him.

Ruth got a mysterious visit from two men claiming to be from the FBI. She said, 'They opened and closed their identification very fast. They said they wanted to come in and look through the house. They never said what they were looking for, and to this day, I don't know what they were looking for.' They tore her house apart but didn't leave with anything.

Investigative journalist Don Devereux didn't believe that Charles had committed suicide and started looking into the unusual case. He uncovered that Charles had been involved in billions of dollars of gold and platinum transactions for the purposes of money laundering between 1973 and his death in 1977. These dealings allegedly also involved CIA agents, Department of Defense agents, and even ex-government officials from Vietnam who were said to have profited greatly from the Vietnam War.

Devereux also uncovered that Charles had used his position as an escrow agent to help Mafia crime boss Joseph Bonanno with shady real estate deals. Devereux found that Charles had kept detailed copies of all his transactions, possibly intending to hand them over to the government as part of his undercover Secret Service duties. It is possible that someone in Bonnano's organization knew that Charles was keeping these records and needed to dispose of him before he did anything with them.

It certainly seemed like Devereux had uncovered some dangerous truths.

On May 14, 1990, Doug Johnston left his home in Phoenix at around 11 p.m. to work a night shift at a computer graphics company. He was later found dead in his car in the parking lot of the building. He had been shot behind the left ear. No gun was found at the scene, and no residue was found on Doug's hands, but this death was also ruled as a possible suicide. The medical examiner said it was either 'self-inflicted, or the work of someone else' with no information on how it could have been a self-inflicted wound if there was no gun found at the scene.

This death is significant not only because of the bizarre ruling, but also because Don Devereux lived right across the street from the parking lot and drove a similar vehicle to Doug Johnston.

After this incident, a fellow journalist told Devereux that Johnston's death was a botched attempt at killing him, and his life was still in danger.

Devereux received a call from another investigative journalist working out of D.C., Danny Casalero. Danny had uncovered corruption in the Justice Department and was looking for Devereux's information on Charles's gold transactions, which would help him link important officials to money-laundering operations.

Only days after his call with Devereux, Danny was found dead in a hotel room bathtub, having slit his wrists twelve times. His family was not notified for two days. When his brother Tony found out how Danny had died, he was immediately suspicious. Danny was famously squeamish when it came to blood and things like needles penetrating his skin. If Danny were to take his own life, Tony didn't believe that he would do it in such a way. He also said Danny had told him about some of his findings and expressed fear that his life was in danger because of what he knew. Danny had told Tony that if he ended up dead, it would not have been by his own hand.

Tony asked the authorities about the documents he knew Danny had had on him the day before. Danny had met an informant who had given him some sensitive information relating to his Justice Department investigation. All these documents were missing from the scene of his death. At least that's what the authorities told Tony.

The hotel room where Danny had died was not treated as a

crime scene, as the death was ruled a suicide. The housekeepers cleaned up the room as normal, potentially destroying evidence that it may have been a murder. One of the cleaning staff later recalled finding blood-stained towels on the floor of the bathroom, indicating that someone may have attempted to stop Danny's bleeding or clean it up.

As for Charles Morgan, Don Devereux has essentially concluded that he was, indeed, an informant for the government, and was simply found out and taken care of before he could compromise any operations. He said, 'There is a great likelihood that Mr. Morgan was, in fact, doing something with the government. I think this was a guy who was extremely naive about a lot of things. I think somebody blew his cover and he got killed.'

Charles's death, as well as those of Doug Johnston and Danny Casalero, remain documented as suicides.

The Axeman of New Orleans

New Orleans, Louisiana is the birthplace of jazz, and today it is a bustling musical city to which people from all walks of life are drawn. Jazz music started in New Orleans's Congo Square, where slaves and immigrants would gather to share the music of their people. The diverse cultures meshed and created a whole new genre of music. Jazz represented a freedom of expression and fluid collaboration between artists that had not been seen before. Jazz was a place of freedom and togetherness. The city itself, though, was not that inclusive.

In the early 1900s, racism ran rampant in the streets of the city. Many Italian immigrants were coming to New Orleans from Sicily. They would initially work on cotton and sugar plantations, among African American and Asian people. They were reviled by the white population for associating with the lower class and experienced similar racism. Even the owners of the plantations they worked on didn't like them much.

Their industriousness meant that they quickly accrued savings to put towards their dreams, quitting their jobs to open their own businesses. This was frustrating for the employers, who wanted their workers chained to the plantation forever.

One plantation owner was quoted as saying the Italians would have 'laid by a little money and are ready to start a fruit shop or grocery store at some cross-roads town.' Basically, they abandoned the plantation to follow their own path, and owners were upset they couldn't exploit their labor anymore.

By the late 1910s, almost half of the town's grocery stores were owned by Italian immigrants. Some believe the tension building between Italians and the racists of New Orleans is what led to the series of gruesome murders in the town from mid May 1918 to late 1919, which came to be known as the Axeman murders. But we have to start almost a decade before these documented Axeman attacks, with a killer known by the press as the Cleaver.

On August 13, 1910, Italian grocers August and Harriet Crutti were menaced in their bedroom by an intruder brandishing a meat cleaver. August was hit with the cleaver, and the couple were robbed. The intruder had come in through the kitchen door, an entry point that would become very familiar to investigators in the coming years. Thankfully, August made a full recovery.

On September 10, 1910, Conchetta and Joseph Rissetto, also Italian grocers, were attacked in their bedroom with a meat cleaver. Again, the intruder had broken in through the kitchen door. Both Rissettos were permanently disfigured but made it out alive. The intruder didn't take any money or valuables, and even left $23 (around $700 in today's currency) behind in the grocery store's register.

In the summer of 1911, Joseph Davi was killed with a cleaver in his bed next to his pregnant wife, Mary. She was asked for money and valuables by the intruder but was too frightened to move. The Cleaver knocked her out, and nothing ended up being taken from the home. It was becoming clear that this person's motive was to terrorize and attack people, not to rob them.

Mary Davi told investigators that the attacker was a white man with an American accent, which puzzled the police, who were certain these killings were the result of the Black Hand, an Italian extortion group sometimes connected to the Mafia, who were often seen terrorizing grocers in the area, demanding money.

The fact that the killer wasn't taking the money and valuables on the premises, and that they were reported to be a white man who definitely didn't have an Italian accent, meant these killings were not Italian-on-Italian crimes. The Black Hand extortions and killings were not always looked into properly, as the authorities didn't want to intrude into Mafia activity. They kind of let the Italian community regulate itself.

After the Davi attacks, the Cleaver stopped his reign of terror for about six years. This may be because he was in jail for a smaller crime, like robbery or trespassing.

In 1917, though, the killings started up again. On December 22, 1917, a Sicilian grocer, Epifanio Andollina, was killed with a hatchet in his bed next to his wife Anna. Again, nothing was stolen. This murder isn't usually attributed to The Axeman, which is a little confusing as it fits the exact profile of the Axeman murders and his killing timeline.

This could have something to do with the turbulent state of the New Orleans Police Department at the time. The police superintendent James W. Reynolds was murdered in 1917 and replaced by Frank Mooney. It is possible that Mooney simply didn't connect older cases to his new work when he joined the NOPD.

In any case, the attack that was first attributed to the Axeman at the time was on May 23, 1918. Joseph and Catherine Maggio, an Italian grocer and his wife, were attacked in their beds with their own axe while they were sleeping. They then had their throats cut with a razor. Catherine's cuts were so vicious she was practically decapitated. Just like the murders attributed to the Cleaver, a slat on their kitchen door had been removed, which is probably how the killer got in and out. Cash totaling $50 was taken from the home, but the intruder also left other cash and valuables, leading the authorities to believe the attack on the Maggios was the main reason he was there.

On June 28, 1918, another grocer, Louis Besumer, and his partner, Harriet Lowe, were found brutally beaten but still alive.

After recovering from the initial shock of the attack, Harriet started accusing Louis of being German and working for the German government. Frank Mooney investigated

Louis as a spy and even detained him for questioning for several days. Harriet was mostly in a daze after the beating. She also accused another man of the attack, before telling Mooney that Louis was the one who attacked her and that he had staged the scene to look like he had also been a victim. Seven weeks after the incident, Harriet ended up dying from complications of her wounds. Though this incident is sometimes reported as being part of the Axeman's attacks, due to Harriet's accusation of Louis, most historians do not believe it to be one of his.

Another attack usually put on the Axeman list is that of Anna Schneider, who was bludgeoned in her bed on August 4, 1918. Anna was attacked with her bedside lamp, and her house was ransacked and burgled. Historians, however, say it does not fit the M.O. of the Axeman. People probably include it because it offers a note of hope: Anna was eight months pregnant at the time and gave birth to a healthy baby girl a week later. It is not known who may have attacked Anna, but it almost certainly wasn't the Axeman.

On August 10, another Italian man, an eighty-year-old barber named Joseph Romano, was attacked. He was found by his nieces, who ran a small grocery out of their home. The women actually saw the attacker and described him as 'dark, tall, heavy-set, wearing a dark suit, and a black slouch hat.' Joseph died two days later.

In the weeks after Joseph's death, three more Italian grocers were robbed, though they weren't attacked with an axe. The Axeman seemed to be ramping up his vendetta.

Newspapers began reporting that people were waiting up, ready to attack the Axeman if he should enter their homes. One report said, 'Armed men are keeping watch over their sleeping families while the police are seeking to solve the mysteries of the ax attacks. Extra police are being put to work daily.'

This seemed to scare the attacker, or perhaps he was once again in jail for pettier crimes, because the attacks stopped for seven months.

Then, on March 9, 1919, a family in Gretna, a city across the river from New Orleans, was brutally attacked. The Italian grocers Charlie and Rosie Cortimiglia, as well as their baby daughter, were assaulted with an axe. The parents survived, but the child did not. Part of their back door was found chipped away, and a bloody axe was found in the backyard.

Despite this crime fitting the profile of an Axeman killing, police were certain it had been committed by a rival grocer family, the Jordanos. The Jordanos had previously given their grocery store to the Cortimiglias, as they thought the elder Jordano, Iorlando, was too old to run it, but the family changed their minds and asked for it back. This caused bad blood between the families, and the Cortimiglias opened a rival store on the same block.

Perhaps the NOPD simply didn't want to believe the Axeman was back in town, so they blamed this attack on the Jordano family.

While in the hospital, Rosie was badgered into implicating Iorlando and his son Frank. They kept asking her leading

THE AXEMAN OF NEW ORLEANS

questions like, 'Frank did it, didn't he?' Once she was discharged from the hospital, Rosie was taken into custody and not allowed to leave until she signed an affidavit saying the Jordanos were responsible for the attack.

The Jordanos were sentenced to prison, and Frank was to be hanged.

Rosie couldn't deal with the guilt of sending two innocent men to prison, so she went to the *Times-Picayune* and asked them to print a retraction of her affidavit. She was threatened with perjury if she didn't stick to her original story, but she insisted she knew it wasn't the Jordanos who had attacked her family. With no further evidence against them, Iorlando and Frank were allowed to go free.

So who *did* attack the Cortimiglia family?

On March 16, 1919, the *Times-Picayune* published a menacing letter from the alleged Axeman of New Orleans. It was postmarked from 'Hell,' and read as follows:

Esteemed Mortal:

They have never caught me and they never will. They have never seen me, for I am invisible, even as the ether that surrounds your earth. I am not a human being, but a spirit and a demon from the hottest hell. I am what you Orleanians and your foolish police call the Axeman.

When I see fit, I shall come and claim other victims. I alone know whom they shall be. I shall leave no clue except my bloody axe, besmeared with blood and brains of he whom I have sent below to keep me company.

149

If you wish you may tell the police to be careful not to rile me. Of course, I am a reasonable spirit. I take no offense at the way they have conducted their investigations in the past. In fact, they have been so utterly stupid as to not only amuse me, but His Satanic Majesty, Francis Josef, etc. But tell them to beware. Let them not try to discover what I am, for it were better that they were never born than to incur the wrath of the Axeman. I don't think there is any need of such a warning, for I feel sure the police will always dodge me, as they have in the past. They are wise and know how to keep away from all harm.

Undoubtedly, you Orleanians think of me as a most horrible murderer, which I am, but I could be much worse if I wanted to. If I wished, I could pay a visit to your city every night. At will I could slay thousands of your best citizens, for I am in close relationship with the Angel of Death.

Now, to be exact, at 12:15 (earthly time) on next Tuesday night, I am going to pass over New Orleans. In my infinite mercy, I am going to make a little proposition to you people. Here it is: I am very fond of jazz music, and I swear by all the devils in the nether regions that every person shall be spared in whose home a jazz band is in full swing at the time I have just mentioned. If everyone has a jazz band going, well, then, so much the better for you people. One thing is certain and that is that some of your people who do not jazz it out on that specific Tuesday night (if there be any) will get the axe.

Well, as I am cold and crave the warmth of my native

Tartarus, and it is about time I leave your earthly home, I will cease my discourse. Hoping that thou wilt publish this, that it may go well with thee, I have been, am and will be the worst spirit that ever existed either in fact or realm of fantasy.

– The Axeman

On the night of March 19, 1919, the whole town played jazz. Clubs stayed open all night, and people hosted parties in their homes where jazz was played constantly.

Interestingly, most experts on the case don't think the Axeman wrote the letter. Historian Miriam Davis, who wrote a book on the case, said:

When you read the letter, this is a person who's an educated person ... The person who is the Axeman, from the descriptions we've got of him, he's a working man, he's working class ... I just don't think a working class person at that time would have been educated enough to write that letter.

Many detectives and criminal profilers agree. The Axeman was most likely lower class, and exhibited frenzied, angry attacks that were not usual for a measured and intelligent person.

Davis points the finger for the letter at jazz musician Joseph John Davilla, who wrote 'The Mysterious Axman's Jazz (Don't Scare Me Papa)' and used newspaper ads referencing the letter, and the night of terror that sprang from it, to advertise his music.

Even the press at the time was shocked that the *Times-Picayune* had published the letter without investigating whether it did actually come from the Axeman. The *West Bank Herald* admonished the *Times-Picayune* for fear mongering and publishing something they knew would cause a stir among the uneducated, lower classes. They wrote:

> Undoubtedly, the letter made good Sunday reading for those who like to read articles of a sensational character, but we must stop to think of the great amount of harm it has done to the ignorant classes who are superstitiously inclined and believed to a certain extent that this ax-man would visit certain families who did not have a jazz band . . . If the *T.-P.* would have devoted the same amount of space in an effort to capture the man who is causing these murders, it would have served the public to a much greater advantage than the publishing of this joke-letter, which caused a great deal of uneasiness and worry among the ignorant classes.

Another killing that is often thought to be part of the Axeman slayings happened in October 1919 when Esther and Mike Pepitone were attacked. Mike died after eighteen strikes with an axe, but Esther, who survived the attack, said there were two men in the room that night. Evidence points to the Pepitone killing being a Mafia hit, or the work of a disgruntled business partner, and not actually that of the Axeman.

Whether or not it was written by him, the real Axeman seemed to keep the letter's promise anyway. No attacks that can be definitively linked by historians to the Axeman were carried out after that jazzy night.

The Ibadan Forest of Horror

In 2014, one of the worst crimes against humanity was uncovered in the Nigerian state of Ibadan.

A motorcycle taxi driver by the name of Abakuda got a call from an acquaintance asking him to drive him to the Soka neighborhood of Ibadan. Abakuda then disappeared. The next day, the other motorcyclists he hung around with desperately searched for him. They recruited his family to help them look, but nobody could find him.

During the search, one of his family members got a call from Abakuda. He said he didn't know where he was, but he felt like he was underground and may have been buried alive. He told them he had been on his way to the Soka forest the night before and had been jumped.

His friends and family all went to Soka to look for him. One of the party saw what looked like a motorcycle in the river. It was Abakuda's. The group continued to search around the area of the river. Some of the men noticed a compound of buildings up a hill in the distance and went to check them out. As they approached, they heard anguished screams and desperate pleas for someone to bring water.

The men were shot at from one of the buildings in the compound, and they fled, but only to retrieve the rest of the party and bring them to this suspicious place to keep searching for Abakuda.

As many as one hundred people arrived at the compound to investigate the cries, and try and find Abakuda.

One of the motorcyclists got a call from the missing man while they searched, saying he could hear people walking above him.

As the party scoured the compound, they came across the most atrocious things they had ever seen. One building housed several prisoners who had been chained to walls and large cement blocks. They were disoriented and emaciated. The men set about freeing the prisoners and most simply fled into the forest, clearly still afraid of whoever was keeping them there.

Another building on the compound housed hundreds of personal items belonging to men, women, and children. Clothing, bags, shoes, wallets, and I.D. cards littered the floor.

Yet another building contained a massive pile of dead bodies. An estimated fifty decaying corpses were found in a heap in the building. In the surrounding area, the party also discovered the fresh remains of twenty more humans and more than a hundred skulls, and countless dismembered body parts were scattered across the site and the forest.

Abakuda stayed in touch with his friends, and told them that he could still hear people walking around above him. Eventually, his phone ran out of batteries, and the lifeline went dark. The property would need to be carefully excavated if they were to have any hope of ever finding Abakuda alive.

By this point, the police had been notified of the search party's gruesome findings, and the Ibadan townspeople had heard about the atrocities of the Soka compound. People started showing up, desperate to either help, find their missing loved ones, or just see the unholy sight for themselves.

The scene was extremely hectic. People were pointing fingers at everyone. The guards who had shot at the search party had not been identified and nobody was sure if they were still there, hiding, if they had fled the area, or if they had blended into the crowd of rescuers. At one point, a small group of men with guns were suspected to be the shooters and were being harassed by the townspeople, but police insisted they were on their side.

There were stories of madmen running around with dismembered ears hanging off their bodies and of malnourished people wasting away in the bushes that surrounded the compound. One man collapsed and died in front of his rescuers.

As more and more people poured into the site demanding answers, the authorities started pushing back and asking them to leave. The scene was pure chaos. Riots broke out as the military descended on the site and refused to let people look for any signs of their missing friends and family. One source says the crowd set a man on fire who they thought was responsible for the atrocities.

One person who knew of Abakuda's plight said, 'We want to rescue our people who are still underground and crying for help, but police are saying no, and we are angry.'

The police and military continued to refuse entry to the townspeople. They even shot into the crowd, attempting to control the madness, and several people died. People in nearby houses and businesses were also terrorized by the angry mob.

The people who had initially been looking for Abakuda could easily hear the cries of the prisoners from outside the buildings. How could the neighbors of the compound not have heard, seen, or smelled anything?

It turned out that they *had* questioned the buildings and the horrific noises coming from them, and had been told that the compound was a mental institution. They were told that the anguished cries were from extremely mentally ill patients.

One source even says that representatives were sent to the compound to ask questions, and the leader, a man with tribal face tattoos, had confirmed that it was a mental institution. He even gave them a tour, where they saw as many as a hundred people squatting in the rooms in one of the buildings, but didn't see any dead bodies, body parts, or signs of torture.

Forensic experts were called by the police to investigate the compound and collect whatever evidence they could.

However, by the time they arrived, the government had already started tearing down the buildings on the site. Townspeople pleaded with officials to excavate underground, or at least stop demolishing the site before any real investigation could be done, but the destruction went on.

The government's hasty actions led most people to believe that it was involved in the crimes and didn't want anyone discovering anything incriminating.

While most of the approximately thirty people who were rescued from the site had fled after their chains were cut, six people were sent to local hospitals. Only a few ever told the stories of their time in the camp.

Cecilia Obiakena, who was seventy-two at the time of her rescue, was initially unable to speak. When she had recovered and her relatives came to get her, it was discovered that she had been missing since 2008. She lived more than five hours' drive away, in Edo state. She had left the house to go to the market six years prior to the discovery of the horrors and had never returned.

Nafio Shittu, another survivor, said he was picked up in his town by people dressed as government officials. They had shoved him into a van and taken him straight to the Soka compound where he remained for seven months.

A woman known as Titi said she was taken from right outside of her house by official-looking people who said they need to talk to her. She and Nafio both said that new victims were brought in every single day. They both confirmed that they never saw anyone actually murdered, but frequently witnessed bodies being carried out of the building where they were kept.

What was the purpose of this hideous place? Most think it was selling body parts for ritualistic practices or harvesting organs for sale on the black market. But that doesn't explain why some people were kept there for months, or even years. It also offers no explanation as to why so many dismembered body parts were found simply scattered around the grounds, or why some corpses were dismembered, but at least twenty were kept intact and thrown into a pile.

Were the perpetrators looking for something specific in their victims? Why were some people kept for so long? Why were some decapitated, or dismembered, but others weren't? Why was Abakuda kept underground, and how many more were buried alive under the compound, never even searched for by the government?

There may never be any answers to these horrific questions. Abakuda was never found, and the site of the atrocities is now a school, which was probably built over his dead body.

Ahmad Suradji, The Killer Shaman

Ahmad Suradji was born on January 10, 1949 in Aman Damai, North Sumatra, Indonesia. He was the ignored and neglected son of the village's shaman. Ahmad's father was greatly respected in the town and didn't have the time to dote on him.

Ahmad acted out early. He did not do well in school and didn't have any friends. He left home at nineteen and immediately got arrested for petty crime and violence. He spent ten years in prison before he was thirty years old. When he was released, he went right back to a life of crime and was back in prison within two years for cattle theft.

Once he was released, Ahmad vowed to change his reputation. He decided he wanted to follow in his now-deceased father's footsteps and become a shaman.

Ahmad became known as Datuk Maringgi, an honorific denoting his importance in society. People genuinely believed

Ahmad had special powers that could help them with relationship, financial, and other personal issues.

In 1986, Ahmad claimed to have had a dream in which his father told him he needed to collect and consume the saliva of seventy women to reach immortality. He set about killing women to achieve this goal, just to speed up the process.

Later he said, 'My father did not specifically advise me to kill people, so I was thinking it take ages if I had to wait to get to seventy women. Because I was trying to get to it as fast as possible, I used my own initiative to kill.'

For the next eleven years, Ahmad used his authority in the community to kill women and get closer to his goal. His position as a shaman who would perform mildly embarrassing rituals for women meant that victims would come to him voluntarily, and most of the women who came to see him wouldn't tell their friends and family where they were going. Ahmad would claim he could do rituals to make women more beautiful and desirable, plus do things like ensure their boyfriends wouldn't leave them for other women. Though there were as many as eighty women reported missing from nearby villages, Ahmed was never suspected. As a Datuk he was far too revered in the community to be suspected of harming people, which allowed him to fly under the radar for so long.

He charged between $200–400 for each ritual. He would take his victim into the sugarcane field near his house. She would help him dig a hole that was about waist deep. The woman would get into the hole and, with her arms by her sides, Ahmad would bury her until she was unable to move. He would then strangle her to death with a cord and collect her saliva. After she was dead, he would dig her up, strip her naked so she would 'decompose faster,' and re-bury her whole body, with her head pointing toward his house.

On April 27, 1997, a farmer was walking his livestock through the sugarcane field that Ahmad used for his rituals. He stumbled across an unusual mound of soil that looked oddly disturbed. He informed the village head, Sugito, of his strange discovery. Sugito gathered a group of men to investigate the mound. When they dug into the soil, they were hit with the unmistakable smell of decay.

According to the authorities, Ahmad joined the men who were digging up the corpse in the field and asked questions about what was going on.

The authorities were called, and the body was identified as twenty-one-year-old Sri Kemala Dewi. Dewi's mother, Arsanah, was called to identify the body of her daughter, who had been missing for three days.

She said, 'It was like my worst nightmare had come to life. I refused to believe it was her, but there she was, dead in front of me.'

After the discovery of Dewi's body was reported, a rickshaw driver in the area, Andreas Suwito, came forward and said he had given Dewi a ride on April 24 to the Datuk's home. Dewi had apparently gone to Ahmad after a fight with her fiancé. She wanted to make sure he didn't leave her for another woman and was seeking his expertise to keep them together.

Thanks to Suwito's information, Ahmad was investigated. A number of personal items of missing women were found in his home.

Ahmad was arrested and gave a series of disturbing confessions. About Dewi's murder he said, 'That night she was scared because we had to walk through a cemetery to get to the sugarcane field plantation. I told her it was fine, but she insisted that my wife accompany us for the ritual. Dewi was the one who asked for my wife to come along and that was how my wife got to know about the murders.'

The wife he was referring to was named Tumini. Ahmad actually had three wives; one source even said all three were sisters.

Ahmad was arrested on April 30, 1997. After a four-day interrogation, he admitted to killing sixteen women over a period of five years. After the belongings of at least twenty-five women were found on his property, he admitted to murdering a lot more.

He told the authorities of his dream about his father, and the plan to collect the saliva of seventy women. He said he sometimes hired sex workers to kill when business was slow because, although many of his victims came to him, he 'could not wait around' for that to happen.

Eventually, he admitted to all of his murders, saying, 'We are all human beings; we all have our own strengths and weaknesses. If I remember correctly, I have murdered forty-two women. I did not suspect I was going to get caught. I did not try to run away when I saw the police because I was resigned to my fate.' He also said it was an 'easy way' to make money, as he would take his victims' payments for his services, then take anything else they had on them after he killed them.

The sugarcane field was thoroughly searched. Four fresh bodies were able to be identified quickly. The remains of potentially even more than forty-two victims were found, with four never being identified or claimed. The victims ranged in age from eleven to thirty.

There ended up being as many as eighty missing person reports from nearby villages, though it has not been confirmed that Ahmad was responsible for all of them.

Ahmad and his wife Tumini were both arrested. Ahmad was executed by firing squad on July 10, 2008. Tumini received a death sentence as well, but it was later changed to life in prison.

Conclusion

Humans are naturally attracted to the fantastical. We're fascinated by odd things that go against the grain and don't quite fit in; by one-in-a-million tales of people who beat the odds or experience inexplicable things.

We like to be reassured that the routine of our everyday lives could be broken at any moment, and something truly amazing could happen to us. It seems that also works the other way around. The traffic jams caused by rubberneckers slowing down to stare at the scene of a crash prove that humans are also drawn to the gruesome, the horrific, and the traumatic.

As a lover of true crime, you know that the weirder the case, the better. We long for twists and turns, surprise reveals, truly terrifying details, a million suspects, or an eerie lack of any leads at all. We want to know about anything that keeps a case from being tediously straightforward.

But why exactly are we so interested in learning about horrific crimes like the ones in this book? Surely we should all want to turn away from the awful tales of such deeply traumatic events.

Psychiatrist Dr. David Henderson says, 'Witnessing violence and destruction, whether it is in a novel, a movie, on TV or a real-life scene playing out in front of us in real time, gives us the opportunity to confront our fears of death, pain, despair, degradation and annihilation while still feeling some level of safety.'

Basically, it primes our brains to be prepared for the worst-case scenario. We get to explore how we would react to the unthinkable without actually having to go through it. We ask ourselves whether we would truly be ready to fight for our lives if something like that were to happen to us. We subconsciously prepare to save ourselves.

As fascinating as strange crimes can be, this collection of stories certainly makes me glad that truly bizarre crimes aren't as common as your run-of-the-mill murders. It seems impossible that one would ever be fully able to face the idea of someone living in their walls, of spirit possession, the desire to consume human flesh, or the disturbing reality of ritualistic killings. Hopefully, after reading this book, we're all at least a little more prepared to deal with the truly bizarre things that go on in this vast and sometimes terrifying world.

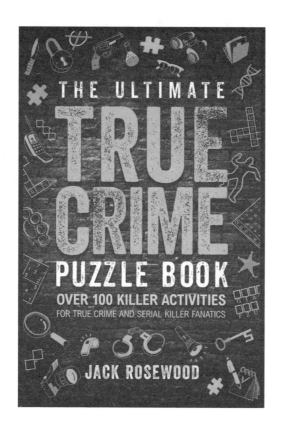

The ultimate puzzle book for
True Crime lovers, from the bestselling author
of *The Ultimate Serial Killer Trivia Book*. Put your mind
to the test to complete over 100 activities – from word
searches and crosswords to riddles and cryptograms –
and learn things you never knew about the
world's most infamous serial killers.

MORE BOOKS BY JACK ROSEWOOD

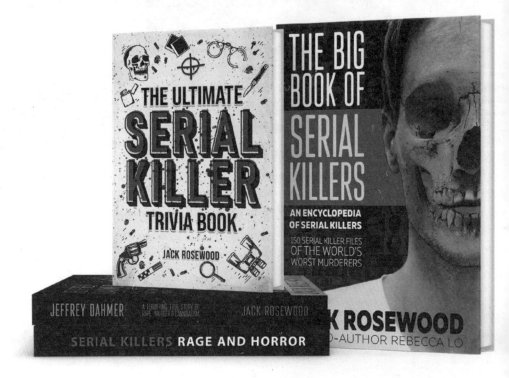

HERE ARE SOME OTHER TITLES YOU MIGHT LIKE:

- Jeffrey Dahmer: A Terrifying True Story of Rape, Murder & Cannibalism

- The Big Book of Serial Killers: 150 Serial Killer Files of the World's Worst Murderers

- Serial Killers Rage and Horror Volume 2: 8 Shocking True Crime Stories of Serial Killers and Killing Sprees

- The Ultimate Serial Killer Trivia Book: A Collection of Fascinating Facts and Disturbing Details About Infamous Serial Killers and Their Horrific Crimes

BUT WE'VE GOT MANY MORE! GET TWO TRUE CRIME BOOKS FOR FREE!

Check out all of our titles at **www.jackrosewood.com**